£12.99

D0256495

# Lessons on the Lunge
## for Horse and Rider

# Lessons on the Lunge
## For Horse and Rider

## MOLLY SIVEWRIGHT
### F.I.H., F.B.H.S., F.A.B.R.S.

798.2

WARD LOCK

# A WARD LOCK BOOK

First published in the UK 1996
by Ward Lock
Wellington House
125 Strand
LONDON
WC2R 0BB

A Cassell Imprint

First paperback edition 1998
Reprinted 1998
Reprinted 2000

Distributed in the United States
by Sterling Publishing Co., Inc.
387 Park Avenue South, New York, NY 10016–8810

A British Library Cataloguing in Publication Data block
for this book may be obtained from the British Library
ISBN 0 7063 7696 X

Typeset by Penny Mills
Photographs by Kit Houghton
except for p.64 by Pattie Curtis.

Printed and bound in Great Britain by
The Bath Press, Bath

# Contents

# Introduction

I have always found the subject of lungeing fascinating. I first became intrigued when my mother taught me how to lunge my very naughty 12.2 hands high Dartmoor pony called Merrylegs. Both he and she taught me a great deal. My mother was extremely particular that every little detail was correct and Merrylegs was the best escapologist in the business! His trump card was produced in moments of boredom when he would come to a slithering stop, turn in to face me, roll his eyes and stand straight up on his two hind legs, clapping his 'hands' and thus entwining both of them through the rein so that when he descended to the ground he had achieved a kind of 'cat's cradle', and would then stand with a smug grin while it took me five minutes to sort everything out again!

Much as Merrylegs' sense of humour gave me an insight into the fun of lungeing, it was the perfectionist streak in my mother's training that has stood me in good stead all my life and I suppose it is this fact combined with the slackening standards of present-day lungeing that urged me on to accept with alacrity Alison Goff of Cassell's invitation to write this book on lungeing in conjunction with Kit Houghton, who is such a wizard with a camera.

The aim of the book is to improve horses, riders, instructors, trainers and lungers; to develop the form of the first and the skills of the others. I hope that the contents will prove to be thought-provoking and beneficial to all horsemen and women and that aspiring lungers as well as those with considerable experience will find something of value within these pages.

As so much of my life's work has been dedicated to training the younger generation to become first-class riding instructors, inevitably I have included information and practical hints for them throughout the book, and I believe such additions will enrich the text for less experienced readers.

I have been fortunate in my equestrian career and perhaps, before expounding my theories, I should explain my own equestrian background more thoroughly.

My mother was taught to lunge horses by her favourite uncle, who was a fine horseman – he won the King's Cup for showjumping and later commanded his regiment, the 3rd Hussars. In turn, my mother taught me to enjoy lungeing my pony, and to become proficient in the methods she herself had learned. What I was taught in those far-off days has stood the test of time. Exactly these same methods have been tested and proved by countless horses in many countries since those early days.

What has been so fascinating and of great importance to me as an instructor, trainer and an author of text books, is that along my life's route I have had frequent and regular opportunities to discuss the details of the methods, backed by practical demonstrations, with top instructors of the Federations of Sweden, Germany, France, Italy and the USA as well as with the 'chiefs' of the Spanish Riding School of Vienna. Of these the person who gave the most of his time and expertise was Major Boltenstern — a rider-instructor and inter-national dressage judge, who won three Olympic gold medals, two silver and one bronze for Sweden. He was invited to run official British Horse Society dressage courses in four centres in England by Colonel V.D.S. Williams, on Colonel Alois Podhajsky's recommendation as 'the finest instructor and trainer in the world — if you can persuade him to leave Stromsholm' (then the Swedish Cavalry School of which Major Boltenstern was the chief in-structor). Major Boltenstern returned to the UK for three further years as the official dressage trainer, after which he came over to our school at Talland once or twice a year for twenty-two years.

During these same years at Talland we also had regular visits and discussion days with General Viebig and Herr Hans Handler from Germany and Herr Rockawansky from the Spanish Riding School of Vienna, and I had the privilege of riding with Colonel Gustaf Nyblaeus and Major Hans Wikne of Sweden, Mr Gunnar Anderson of Denmark and Colonels Podhajsky and Handler and Herr Bachinger from the Spanish Riding School. All of these great instructors had a wonderful depth of knowledge based on years of experience with hundreds if not thousands of horses and pupils, and all of them were most generous with their interest and time in discussing training principles and techniques. None was jealous, each was keenly interested to hear of the others' methods and ideas, and for myself this was a wonderful way to establish the British system of horse-training, from handling upwards — naturally and without force. I was thrilled, delighted and greatly relieved to find that in each case there was mutual agreement with official substantiation from each country's equestrian manuals. Not only were the methods identical but we also shared the same aims:

- safety
- improvement by natural means
- ease of understanding
- ease and efficiency of use.

Lungeing is often regarded as a rather mundane chore. It is not unusual to hear the suggestion that the horse be given about half an hour on the lunge in order ' . . . to get the tickle out of his toes', or ' . . . to give him some exercise before you go off for the day', or ' . . . because he had a hard day yesterday', or ' . . . until his sore back or girth-gall has recovered enough to put a saddle on and ride him again', or ' . . . until he is sound'. Yes, believe it or not, the last has been given as a purpose for lungeing, qualified by ' . . . well, he's got to be kept fit, he's entered for a competition next week — there's no weight on his legs when he is lunged'. In this last instance, the horse did not compete — he was ordered to have six weeks' box-rest, followed by four weeks walking exercise and *no* lungeing! Of course, some of these objectives are valid, providing that the lunger knows how to work the horse correctly and well on the lunge.

Sometimes lungeing is raised above this 'chore' level to that of a cure-all training aid for problem horses or for those whose owners have goals which they must achieve . . . yesterday! This category of 'trainer' can do more lasting damage to a horse than those in the first-mentioned category because they employ forceful means to try to improve upon nature too quickly. These people try to force a horse into submission and a desired outline by using harmful and cruelly restricting methods, such as side reins adjusted far too tight, ' . . . to *pull* the horse's head in', or by tightening the inner side rein, ' . . . to *make* the horse bend to the inside'.

In Australia I was told of a horse who was pronounced by his owner to be 'stiff to the right' and whose cheek snaffle rein had been tied to the roller so tightly that the horse's head was facing backwards to the right and there he was left in the paddock for the night. Barbaric treatment such as this smacks of the Dark Ages of horsemanship rather than logical training carried out by an intelligent human being of the twentieth century.

As a Chief Examiner of the British Horse Society, for many years I have been most concerned at the poor standard of lungeing and the high proportion of candidates who have failed miserably in this section of the instructor's examinations, at all levels. Similarly I have been alarmed by the number of horses who have been abused by self-appointed 'trainers', horses who have been 'trained' to be confused or even downright nappy by so-called 'lunge training' of a dismal quality or who have been tortured by forceful gadgets which have no place in classical equine training and which are only used in an attempt to replace the trained lunger's skills.

I am sure readers will have heard of these gadgets, which their creators claim will improve the horse's outline. Some do it by fixing a heavy weight to the horse's head, under his chin; others by tying the horse's head down with a solid rein fixed tightly to the bit at the front end, passing under his trunk and tied to his tail at the back end. Research has revealed a possible source for the latter evil gadget: the method was employed in battle by the ancient Egyptians, who tied down the heads of their chariot horses in order that their skulls would act as a bony shield and protect their hearts, which were regarded as the engines of the warriors' war-machines. It seems that those warriors did not realize the positioning or the value of the horse's brain!

Those are nightmare situations which should have died years ago. Hopefully enlightenment will lead to their speedy extinction.

All training of horses has to be based on solid foundations, i.e. on a system which is as safe as possible, which is classical in that it has proved through the test of time to be the best, which is logical and which reflects a deep, genuine love of the horse.

The main rules to follow when training horses are those of reward and correction. Of the two, *reward* must have the greater emphasis as it is so important that the horse understands fully and immediately when he has pleased his trainer by performing good work; his trainer's well-timed encouragement will guarantee sure progress. Spare a moment to imagine yourself as a beginner pupil learning an entirely new sport such as ice skating and being expected to join a class which is already quite skilled at skating figures; it is easy to understand how much more quickly you would progress being taught by a coach who is logically clear and calmly encouraging than if you were taught by one who is brusque and arrogant with an aggressive manner and who is intolerant of the smallest of mistakes. So it is with a horse.

If you study how other animal trainers operate, it is interesting to see what an important factor is reward. The animals are given liberal additional rewards such as meaty titbits for dogs and tigers, sugar lumps for liberty horses and fishy ones for water-loving animals. It is sad that this practice is not more evident in all trainers of the equine species. Unfortunately for our horses and ponies, the rewards of genuine praise and an accompanying titbit are often overlooked. Many horse trainers are too short-tempered and too stingy with their rewards, which their horses clearly reflect in their attitude and expressions.

The reader may ask, 'How do I know whether an instructor or trainer is well

*The horse understands fully and immediately when he has done well from his trainer's well-timed encouragement, which will guarantee sure progress.*

4

trained?' To this question my answer would be to find out if he or she has a national qualification; if he has a reputation as a good lunger and also to check if his horses have good gaits and work in a good form with a happy and interested expression.

Although lungeing a horse may seem at first sight to be a simple task, in fact to lunge a horse well takes a lot of skill. Even lungeing an experienced horse for exercise can be dangerous for both the lunger and the horse if the former has not had sufficient training in this all-important subject.

Similarly, lunge lessons can be most beneficial to riders who wish to improve their riding skills and/or who require help to overcome well established bad habits. Here again, I must add the criteria that the lunger must be well trained. Not only must he or she have a good eye and feel for the horse he is lungeing, but also he must have been trained to develop quick, X-ray eyes which enable him to see from his position in the centre of the circle when the rider slides to the outside, when he grips with his thighs, over-tenses the muscles around his hips, in his back, his shoulders, arms, neck, feet or whenever unwanted excess tension abounds. He should understand the value of teaching his pupil how to ask for and achieve good smooth yet forward-going transitions rather than over-taxing the rider with endless trotting accompanied only by occasional monotone commands or a veritable barrage of instructions. The lunger who has the privilege of working a rider *and* a horse should always endeavour to inspire both of them for their improvement.

*Terminology*

As an instructor myself, I believe it is very important that words and phrases are used which will precisely communicate their meaning. There are three phrases used in this book which are worthy of a short explanation:

1. The gaits of the horse as opposed to the 'paces'. Antique text books written by veterinary and equestrian masters and all present day veterinary experts and dictionaries agree with the use of the noun gait to describe a 'manner of walking or going, carriage', to do with footfalls of walk, trot, (canter) and gallop.

I do not know where 'paces' came from – I always hope I never have to ride a horse who does it! Scholars of the English language will find it interesting to note that according to authentic English dictionaries a pace is defined variously as, from Roman times, 'the space between the feet from one heel to the next, an amble, rate of speed or progress, to go very fast'. When I suggested we should lead the way with paces corrected to gaits, I was told we should wait for the F.E.I. (the international governing body) to make the change.

2. 'In a good form' as opposed to 'having a good outline'. I prefer to use the former because it means far more than does the latter term. If a horse is in a good form it means the outline is correct because he moves well in all his gaits, he uses all his muscles with supple ease, power and impulsion, he is on the bit and works under his rider willingly, happily and with pride.

Thus the phrase 'in a good form' is used to refer to the whole of the horse, from his brain, spinal cord and nervous system, his skeletal structure, his internal organs and his vast musculature, from the deepest muscles of the horse, layer by layer, to the glossy coat on the outermost surfaces. The trained eye of an equestrian expert will be able to make accurate assessments of all these factors as he assesses and evaluates each horse's confidence, balance, suppleness, physique and his way of going. On the other hand, the phrase 'a good outline' is apt to produce a mental picture of a single line drawn on see-through paper around the outside edges of a stationary or moving but flat horse.

The observer, whether judge or lunger, has a myriad of desirable qualities to assess when he looks to see if a horse is working 'in a good form', whereas he only has to define a tracing of the horse's silhouette if he is looking for 'a good outline'.

3. 'Starting' young horses in their training rather than 'breaking them in'. Personally, I have an intense dislike for the latter term – it conjures up barbaric scenes where the young horse is captured from his wild, free state and is submitted to previously unknown and terrifying attacks by loud, rough human beings until he is mentally and physically exhausted and his spirit broken, submits to the saddle tied fast on his back, and to commands of the rider sitting masterfully on top of that saddle. I have known of three good and valuable young horses who were killed in one year alone by quick, careless and thoughtless methods of 'breaking-in', none of which were at Talland I hasten to add. At Talland we have used the term, 'Starting the training of young horses' for the past twenty years; I believe it explains exactly what we do and I was delighted to hear the 'starting expert', Monty Roberts, use exactly the same term when he came to England several years ago. I hope that thinking equestrian experts will join me in a crusade against 'breaking-in', in theory and in practice.

For ease of expression, I have referred to the horse throughout the book as he, and to the rider, lunger, instructor as either he or she. The information and instruction of course applies equally to both sexes – human and equine.

# 1

# Good Beginnings

## THE PURPOSES OF LUNGEING

1. To give riders an additional dimension to the training and development of the horses with whom they are working. The psychological aspect of lungeing should be appreciated from the start; as the trainer's mental and physical presence and strength can be felt and seen so clearly by the horse, his trainer is able to create a strong telepathic bond and an ever-increasing confidence and trust.

2. For young horses – when they are being started. (No, *not* 'broken in' – that has to be one of the worst terms still in use in the English equestrian language for it implies that horses are trained by cruel, ignorant, spirit-breaking methods, whereas hopefully that is no longer the case.)

3. As an initial introduction to young horses of a very new way of life, i.e. being trained to work and to accept direction to suit human tasks. It is an excellent means of introducing young horses to the new concept – accepting the trainer's presence, listening to his thoughts, watching his movements, learning his ways, and complying with his wishes.

4. Work on the lunge helps to get the young horse physically fit; his musculature is developed so that he is ready to carry the weight of a rider, to pull a vehicle or for whatever other extraordinary tasks may lie ahead.

5. To give horses exercise – lungeing is very useful for this purpose especially if the horse has a girth gall, a warble or small, hard lump coming up under the saddle area or some such problem which prevents him from carrying a saddle or harness. There are also times when the trainer, rider or driver may not be able to ride or drive.

6. It is a safe way of assessing a strange horse's temperament, manners and movement, providing this is done by a competent lunger.

7. It provides a useful opportunity to be able to observe the horse working from the ground with a side view of his expression, his form, balance and gaits.

8. To improve the horse's way of going – it is very easy to help the horse to be more supple, to use his musculature and to move with greater ease for all his joints when he is worked on a lunge-line or long reins by an expert, untrammelled by a rider-burden.

9. Lungeing is a safe way to introduce a horse to new surroundings – a young or excitable horse can be calmed before he

competes at a horse show or competition, in the least taxing way for both horse and rider. After a short spell of good work on the lunge, inevitably he will be more confident, supple and calm, ready for his rider. The lunger must never lunge at a competition without asking permission and he must be very courteous to all riders who are working their horses in the same area.

10. To start the retraining of a spoiled horse.

11. To prepare a horse for a side saddle before the rider rides him.

12. To improve the rider's balance, confidence, posture and suppleness, and to encourage the correct use of the seat and therefore improve the rider's influences on the horse. From this comes a better understanding of the six natural aids (see page 14) helped by the contact, control and concentration of the instructor.

13. Restoring a rider's nerve after some unfortunate incident, or building confidence with a new horse, especially with an adult beginner who feels, albeit mistakenly, that to be put on a leading-rein would be an insult to his dignity.

14. Lungeing is extremely useful when training and preparing small ponies for children. A good lungeing session will instil and refresh obedience as well as removing the tickle out of their toes and rendering them safer for their jockeys.

**THE RISK FACTOR**

As with all activities connected with horses, several factors should be borne in mind before any untrained person embarks on what may seem to him or her to be 'such an easy task that it is not worth bothering about'.

It must be appreciated and remembered that at all times work around and with horses is of a high-risk nature. Horses are large, strong and heavy creatures with minds of their own. They are extremely sensitive and often pick up thoughts and actions which a human may not even realize he has made. Once a horse reaches a state of panic it is often impossible to make him understand that you did not mean what you thought or did, and that it was all a huge mistake. Usually horses appear to be kind and docile, and indeed most of them are. However, the known fact that all horses are unpredictable must be stressed frequently as inexperienced people have no idea how potentially dangerous all horses are due to their great size, strength, weight and latent agility.

Untrained lungers will also be unsuspecting but they should not have to suffer severe injuries such as broken limbs, backs or skulls in order to appreciate the hazards of this occupation. Any horse at any time may be triggered off into a state of blind panic by a sudden reminder of one or more incidents of bad treatment in his past; he may be frightened by some strange sight, sound or smell, or he may be spooked for no apparent reason. If a horse panics he can be transformed immediately into an extremely dangerous if not lethal animal. 'To be forewarned is to be forearmed' — after a would-be lunger has lost fingers or a thumb or suffered worse injuries, it is too late to wish he had invested more time, money and energy in training.

The risk factor in working with horses is heightened even more during lungeing sessions due to the length of the lunge-rein, which makes mental and physical contact with the horse so much more remote; it also increases the horse's opportunity to use his great strength to his advantage and possibly to escape. A loose horse with a trailing lunge-rein can be dangerous to himself and to anybody else he may encounter as he flees.

So here comes a word of warning: before attempting to lunge a horse or a pony for any purpose whatsoever, go and learn how to lunge correctly, first on your feet with a friend on his or her feet, then under instruction with a reliable lunge horse. Only after these two steps have been achieved satisfactorily should you progress to learning how to lunge a half-trained pony (they are small, quick and testing and they can advance your lungeing skills quite considerably, providing you can meet their challenge!). Learn or revise the feel of being lunged on a horse yourself before learning how to lunge a rider on a horse, and then learn how to start a young horse on the lunge. In these ways you will find out just how much there is to learn – it is all so interesting, and every horse will teach you some new facet.

You will need a qualified instructor or trainer to teach you exactly how to lunge well. It is a mistaken economy to be misled by a well-meaning friend who tells you that they have lunged a pony or two and that they will teach you how it is done. The quality of the instructor's training can be judged by the seniority of the certificates he or she holds. It stands to reason that the best teachers of the craft or art of lungeing will most probably be found in a riding establishment which is approved by the national governing equestrian body.

## CHOOSING AN ESTABLISHMENT – AND AN INSTRUCTOR/TRAINER

It is relatively easy for a lay person who does not possess a list of nationally approved riding schools to judge whether or not a school will come up to standard, if the following pointers are taken into account:

• Look for a notice board displaying a certificate of approval from the national governing body.

• Efficiency in the office, a welcoming reception, and the making of sensible enquiries in order to give you or the prospective pupil a lesson which combines safety and progressive education.

• A caring, safe and happy atmosphere in the yard amongst horses, owners, students and staff.

• All the horses and ponies should appear to be well fed, standing with well-shod feet on comfortable beds or clean floors, and they should look happy with ears mainly pricked forward.

• Good maintenance of all the necessary items, such as the saddlery being in good condition, soft and supple, and hanging up neatly in a tidy tackroom; the feedshed, utensils and the surrounding outbuildings and arenas should look clean and workmanlike.

*A very busy yard with many and varied activities taking place simultaneously. Good safety rules and discipline combine to ensure horses and students are happy and safe.*

● The general effect of the establishment should present a picture of being well cared for and efficiently run.

You should walk out quickly from a yard in which you notice any of the following:

● No notice of official approval from a national body.

● An office which looks like the dumping area for a jumble sale.

● Miserable, worried and/or cross-looking faces, human or equine.

● Thin, overworked horses.

● Dirty feedbins and stables, a mucky yard, implements lying around.

● An egg-shaped track in the riding surface of the indoor or outdoor school, denoting low standards of instruction and of maintenance. (The first can be corrected by improved tuition of school figures and variety in the school work, and the second by a rake.)

● Dogs, toddlers and/or poultry running loose in the yard.

● Raucous laughter and abrasive noise, which often warn of danger due to a lack of care and of safety.

Apart from the impressive array of certificates in the office, which confirms the first requirement of an instructor, i.e., that he or she has reached an acceptable standard, of equal importance is the fact that the instructor is a good communicator with whom you can get on well. He or she should be caring, patient, kindly, considerate and courteous, and should have a gift for expressing him- or herself well. A lively sense of humour may not be essential, but it helps! It should be quite evident that the instructor likes horses, people and the work.

A good instructor, who is meticulous and painstaking, should care genuinely for your improvement and be prepared to help you to get a real *feel* for the work, with additional explanations and/or demonstrations as may be necessary to this end.

In addition, the establishment should have good areas and facilities for training and

should display clear evidence of high standards and regard for safety.

All work with horses is of a high-risk category and for this reason all conscientious people who are attending or working at an equestrian establishment should take out their own personal accident insurance cover.

## FACILITIES FOR LUNGEING

Although an indoor riding school is an ideal place in which to lunge, there can be many suitable alternative sites out of doors. The primary factors to bear in mind when viewing a lungeing arena are:

*The lunge area should not be too large or too small. The fencing should be well built with the rails inside the posts and the surface should be level, secure yet springy.*

*The horse should be the right size for the rider!*

1. The area. The ground should be as flat and level as possible. The area should not be too large as that makes it more difficult to keep the horse under control, or too small as then it can be boring – for the lunger as well as the horses.

An area of 20 × 20 m (66 × 66 ft) is a good size for starting a young, untrained horse; a 20 × 40 m (66 × 132 ft) arena is safe and provides more scope for a trained horse.

The lungeing area should not be smaller than 20 × 20 m (66 × 66 ft) or the work has to be too restricted; moving in small circles is both physically taxing and mentally boring. An area which is too small will cause unwanted wear in the horse's joints as well as to the surface itself, and the horse's enthusiasm is bound to wilt. The area should be free from startling distractions.

2. The enclosing fence. This must be constructed of safe material, such as post and rails – not barbed wire as young obstreperous horses can become virtually 'blind' with panic or fear and run into the outer fence. The strength and quality of the fencing will depend on the type of lungeing being carried out; for instance wild young horses require a solid fence, not less than 1.75 m (6 ft) in height, whereas a more placid horse will be quite safe within a temporary construction of bales and poles. Of course, an indoor school is ideal.

3. The footing. This should be comfortable for the horse; it should be springy and secure but not be too deep. It must never be hard, it must not be slippery, stony, inconsistent or uneven as lungeing itself can put extra strain on a horse's joints, ligaments and tendons. If, in addition, the footing is not elastic, secure and level, or if he is worked on too small a circle, i.e., under 12 m (39 ft) in diameter, the extra strain could cause severe or permanent damage.

## THE LUNGE HORSE

### To train the lunger

In order to learn how to lunge it is essential to have a kind and reliable horse who has been well trained to lunge and is responsive, co-operative and sound, who retains an interest in what is going on and who has a forgiving nature. He should not be too large and awe-inspiring, or mentally or physically awkward. A large, well-balanced pony or a cob can prove to be a faithful friend in this respect. If a novice lunger attempts to lunge a young, untrained horse that can be a sure recipe for disaster.

### To teach the rider

The best sort of lunge horse will help novice pupils to learn and improve their riding skills. He should be of the right size for the rider, neither too narrow nor too wide, and have reasonable gaits. He should have a good walk and be 'well connected', with a good swing in his back at trot. He should be well trained for the work, be reliable, interested, sound, and he must have a good temperament.

# 2

# Lungeing Language

Many people think that to lunge a horse is a very simple task. They believe that, 'All you have to do is make him go round and round you, lots of times to the left, and then – if there is time and you can do it – send him lots of times round to the right. And that's it – you've lunged him!' They believe the horse should then be quiet and safe to ride so the target has been reached.

In fact, of course, there is much more to lungeing than that. As with all equestrian tasks, the skills have to be well learned – and well taught too. So much depends on the novice's introduction to lungeing; if potential lungers can be inspired to learn and develop their skills, both they and their horses will gain great benefits and so will their own pupils in due course of time, should they decide to take up teaching.

A rider must have a thorough knowledge and understanding of the *six natural aids* by means of which he or she communicates with the horse:

1. The thought aids (plan, telepathy, awareness)

2. The weight aids

3. The leg aids

4. The rein aids – from the back of the rider's neck and shoulder-blades, through supple joints of shoulders, elbows, wrists, hands and fingers.

5. The voice aids

6. Feel – mental and physical

## THE LUNGER'S AIDS OR SIGNALS

As with riding, the first phase of lungeing must be the introduction of the lines of communication or the lunger's natural aids. The six natural aids used by the rider have to be adapted to suit lungeing. The aids or signals which the trainer or lunger uses to communicate with the horse when he is being lunged are:

1. *The thought aids*. The trainer's telepathy and will, his or her calmness, intelligence, kindness and positive delivery, these combine to form this most important aid. As when riding, the lunger uses his thought aids positively in three ways:

● The plan – basically, it is not wise to lunge into the wing of a show jump or to collide with another horse!

● Telepathy and empathy – it is most important that the ideas, thoughts and mental pictures being projected by the lunger to the horse are reasonable, positive and kind, as well as being simple and clear. It is equally important that the lunger possesses understanding and tact which enable him or her to relate instantly to the horse's thoughts, feelings and needs at each moment.

● Awareness – anyone lungeing a horse must be aware of the presence and safety of other riders, children and so on, who may be moving in the vicinity.

2. *The voice aids.* The tone of the lunger's voice rather than his native tongue is readily translated by the horse. Horses do not worry whether the commands are in English, Swedish, French or German, it is the expression and the tone which they listen to and understand.

The lunger must be consistent with his simple commands; he must enunciate the words clearly without shouting, and endorse their message with sincerity and feeling.

The usual commands for upward transitions are: Walk-on, Trot-on or Terr-ROT and CAN-ter. All of these should be spoken very clearly and if necessary even with a sense of urgency.

The commands for downward transitions are: 'Steady', meaning 'balance yourself, we are going to change down' or 'there is no need to hurry so much', i.e. 'Steady' is the lunger's form of a half-halt. This may be followed by 'Terr-rot', 'Walk' or 'Whoa', spoken in a slow, soothing, drawn-out tone.

Words of praise such as 'Good', 'Good boy' or 'Good girl' must be spontaneous and spoken with utmost sincerity, precisely when deserved.

Although the lunger should maintain a constant communication with the horse he is lungeing, this should be one of quiet and intelligent understanding, a mutual thought process rather than a flow of meaningless chatter.

Tongue-clicking is an adjunct to the lunger's voice aid, which has a remarkably effective forward-driving influence. For this very reason all lungers must be wary of their tongue-clicking, and make sure it is never louder than their own horse requires. Over-loud tongue-clicks can have quite disastrous effects on any other horses who are being worked within hearing distance. Tongue-clicks should be used sparingly to keep the horse responsive to their sound.

3. *Body language.* Horses watch and read the lunger's body language with acute sensitivity. I have seen inexperienced lungers frighten young horses quite inadvertently by, for example, making a jerky movement. The lunger then wonders why the horse rushed round, not realizing that she had lifted her hand to push her hair back or to swat a batch of flies from round her head or had bent down to move a stone underfoot, or to pick up a whip which she had dropped on the ground by mistake.

By placing, positioning or moving him- or herself the lunger can exert a strong influence on the horse. For this reason, he or she must keep working for improvement in posture, poise and subtle strength, and must guard against making false or sudden movements which could be mistranslated by a sensitive horse; similarly lungers must be aware that while controlling excessive gesticulations they must not stifle their natural body language.

When working the horse on a circle, the lunger should move round, with quiet,

*The lunger's aids. These two photographs show them all in use in harmony with the horses, although we cannot hear the quiet and kindly voices. The first horse is feeling exuberant and the lunger's left hand is already on his left hip. The second horse was feeling hot and lethargic half a second earlier. He responds instantly to his trainer's forward-driving aids.*

steady yet nimble footwork, almost on the spot, keeping the line of his shoulders facing a spot just behind that of his horse's shoulders; so that he can maintain concentrated observation of the whole of the horse for all of the time. His feet should be stabilized around the centre point of the circle but ready to be very mobile if necessary. The movements of his upper limbs, firmly based from the back of the shoulder-blades, should be controlled, soft, supple yet firm and unobtrusive, his head should be held tall and back on a strong neck, initiating the strength of his stance.

One of the strongest influences the lunger has is that of stepping forward positively, or even sharply, towards the horse's girth area. This has an immediate forward-driving effect and should only be used sparingly, on a dull horse.

4. *The rein aids*. When lungeing a horse, the rein aids are the major form of control, guidance and restraint. Whereas a rider's base of support depends on his correctly positioned seat bones, the lunger's base of support relies on the firm stance of his feet (except in the direst of moments!). The rein aids themselves are based on the strong muscles and ligaments which originate at the back of the lunger's head and neck to the back of his shoulder-blades which, through connection to the back, the hips and the lower limbs, then tie in with the base of support, i.e. stoutly shod feet.

It is very important that the lunger develops a good, sensitive and supple feel through the whole of his upper limbs and the lunge-rein to make a soft and consistent contact with the lower part of the horse's skull, via the front ring on the cavesson. Sometimes an expert lunger may attach the rein to the bit but that is not included here as it is a much more specialized technique.

5. *The lunger's whip*. This is a substitute for the rider's leg and whip aids. Its primary purpose is to encourage the horse to use his muscles more effectively and efficiently. (See Chapter 4, pages 44–50.)

6. *Feel*. This is just as important for a good lunger as it is for a good rider. Naturally the horse's mental state can be assessed equally well by the lunger or rider, with a slight edge for the lunger because he can see the expression on the horse's face from his vantage point at the side. The rider has the edge over the lunger in the physical aspect as he can feel the horse's movement, ease or tension under his seat. The lunger cannot feel all this in the same way, but he can watch the working of the horse's major trunk muscles, and he can see and analyse their effect on the joints of the horse's limbs and movement extremely well as he views him from the side.

# 3

# Lungeing Equipment

Horses are large, strong and sensitive creatures and thus it is essential that all the items of saddlery are of good quality, light yet strong, well made, well cared for, supple and comfortable. They should of course fit correctly in all areas.

It is important to check every item of saddlery for soundness every day for the safety of the people involved as well as for the horse. If an item of his equipment were to break it would inevitably be very upsetting for a young horse and may cause a major set-back in his training and, of course, such a careless mishap could endanger people too.

*Talland Muschamp Geordano and his lunger ready to go to the lunge area to prepare for his ridden training. But spot the mistake – the jowl strap needs tightening to prevent the cheek strap from rubbing his outer eye. Compare with the photographs on page 20.*

There is a wide variety of equipment available on the market; some of it is useful and much of it is not! It is not necessary to have a saddle-room that is full of lungeing gear; the following items will suffice for all normal lungeing work, from starting the training of a young horse, to improving the training of a mature or a badly trained horse:

## A cavesson

There are many types of cavessons hanging up in saddlers' shops. On the whole they fall into two main categories. One is rather like a glorified headcollar or halter with a jowl strap as well as a throat-lash. A front strap running from the centre of the headpiece lies down the front of the horse's face and holds up the rather weighty noseband which is padded for its entire length. This type is made to be fitted so that the noseband is in the normal position for a cavesson noseband, i.e. it goes around the horse's head, above the bit. Its noseband is too long and cumbersome to be fitted as a drop noseband.

The alternative type, thought to be modern, is in fact the pattern that was universally used by most of the major British and European Cavalry Schools for many years before World War One. This type of cavesson is much lighter in weight as it only has one jowl strap and no throat-lash and no front strap; also the noseband is shorter and is only padded in the front as it is intended to be fitted as a drop noseband under the bit. As it is lighter it is more comfortable and, being positioned lower on the skull, this cavesson has two further obvious advantages:

• It is easier to 'work' the horse's skull to free his poll and thereby enable his trunk muscles to move with greater freedom and mobility.

• The lunger has far greater control over the horse should the latter have a wayward nature.

Both patterns of cavesson have a lightweight, snugly fitting, hinged metal band built into the front section of the noseband, onto which are fixed three metal rings. The jowl strap should be fitted reasonably tightly to prevent the cavesson from slipping out of place as there is then a danger that the outside cheek strap will move forward onto the horse's outside eye.

When doing up the cavesson, care must be taken that the cheek straps of the bridle remain free.

Personally, I prefer and use the second, lightweight cavesson.

Before putting on the cavesson, over and under the bridle, the riding noseband should be removed and put to one side ready to be replaced immediately the lungeing session is finished – unless the riding bridle is fitted with a cavesson noseband and the cavesson itself is of a drop-noseband type. In this case they will not interfere with each other and, if the noseband is left on the bridle, it will not be lost.

A word of warning about the front strap on the more cumbersome cavesson: although theoretically its original aim was to hold up the heavy front part of the noseband, it does hold a hidden danger as I found to my cost, many years ago. The front strap must never be fitted tight enough to support the

*Left: The jowl strap is nearly tight enough. The unpadded back-strap of the noseband is fitted as a drop-noseband under the bit. Right: The jowl strap is correct here – the completely padded noseband is fitted above the bit.*

noseband as in practice, if it is tight and a horse plays up, turns in to face the lunger and then pulls back, this front strap can pull the headpiece forward over the ears with the utmost ease and dexterity!

### A lunge-rein

This should be strong, quite thin and light and approximately 8–10 m (26–33 ft) in length, with a stop at one end and a swivel and spring-clip at the other. If the rein has a loop rather than a stop, it should be used as a stop. It is dangerous to put your hand into the loop – your hand could be trapped and damaged, especially if the horse should run away out of control.

The type of lunge-rein is an individual matter, dependent on the size and feel of the lunger's hand and the environment in which the lungeing is due to take place. The two most usual materials are cotton rope and webbing. I prefer the former.

Nowadays both of these materials often have a small proportion of nylon added, but it is important that the proportion is very small or the rein will not break should an accident occur. Also it will be slippery if it gets wet. The advantages of a rope rein are that it is easier to hold in and release from the hand, and it is better out of doors because the wind does not affect the contact between the trainer's hand and the horse's head. Webbing can rot without a visible warning sign and it does develop quite a disconcerting judder when used out of doors. It is more cumbersome in the air when lungeing horses over fences.

### A lunge or training roller

This should be strong, sound and well padded, i.e., it should have sufficient stuffing on either side of a wide channel so that there is no pressure on the horse's spine.

It should have two or three pairs of 'D' rings fitted exactly level, on each side. The lowest pair of rings should be just about the level of the points of the horse's shoulders and the highest pair 15 cm (6 in) from the top of the roller. A 'D' ring should be fitted to the front and another to the back of the top of the roller, the latter being for the crupper.

The roller should also have a breast girth (strap or plate), which will be needed for a herring-gutted horse – one who has little substance in his middle part – and for all young horses. If he is worked well, the horse will develop the muscles to hold the saddle correctly behind the shoulder-blades and the girth in the girth groove, where the sternum and the ziphoid cartilage join under his chest. Nothing teaches a horse how to buck quicker than a roller or saddle which has slipped back; this has been the cause of many bad accidents and resultant serious injuries to horses and their riders.

### A crupper

This should have three buckles, one on the main strap which goes along the horse's back and one at each side of the padding which goes under his tail; the padded part should have a sheepskin covering to ensure that it does not rub the sides of his buttocks or the underside of his tail.

Young horses should be prepared for this important piece of equipment by wearing a tail bandage for two or three hours in the morning and in the afternoon, for several days before the crupper is introduced, after the horse has been worked for some time in an enclosed place.

As soon as the horse is used to wearing it, the crupper should be fitted quite tightly. This will hold back the roller or saddle to give the horse's shoulders free play and to allow the muscles to develop in front of the roller, which will then keep the saddle back in its correct place, behind the back of the shoulder-blade. A well-fitting crupper in the early days will eliminate the need for a foregirth. Obviously, it is far better to build up muscles to hold back the saddle rather than to have to put on a fixed, mechanical device which inhibits the muscular development as well as the freedom of movement in the horse's shoulders and of the shoulder-blades themselves, forwards and backwards over the horse's rib-cage.

### A saddle

Later in the horse's training, a well-fitting saddle will replace the roller. It should have a wide enough channel to allow plenty of room for the horse's spine, as well as his shoulder-blades and the ligaments and muscles which must have free play on either side of it. The channel must not be too wide or it will not be sufficiently stable on his back. A pair of front-girth straps should be fitted onto well-covered tree points to hold the saddle well back behind the horse's shoulder-blades. Again this is a much more logical and effective method of keeping the saddle back than using a rigid foregirth which is pushed forward into the back of the shoulder-blades and allows no room for the required muscle development behind free shoulder-blades. Foregirths were once thought to be the 'in thing' but I believe the reason to be much more commercial than natural or logical.

### A snaffle bridle

This should fit comfortably and be introduced at an early stage in the horse's training. The bit should be smooth, light and fairly thick, just wide enough for the horse's mouth (5 mm / ¼ in of extra width at each side of his mouth is quite sufficient). The bit should never be too wide or the joint will hang down, weighing on the horse's tongue, and in a very short time he may learn to put his tongue over the bit which is a most tiresome habit to have to cure. Also a too wide snaffle bit will slide over to one side with an uneven and uncomfortable bearing on the horse's tongue and lower jaw. It is unwise to depend on the labelling. My horse, Morning Star, stood 16.2 hands high but was comfortable in bits labelled for a 14.2 pony! Conversely, if the bit is too narrow it will be most uncomfortable for the young horse and will make him 'mouthy'.

To put bridle reins which are sewn onto the bit out of action and out of the way ready for lungeing, the reins should be wrapped once round the horse's neck, after which

a

c

*How to put bridle reins, which are sewn onto the bit, snugly and safely out of the way ready for lungeing.*

*This method is quick and efficient; it is safe for loose jumping and kind to the leather of the reins.*

the reins can be given one turn around each other, quite close to the bit, before passing the throat-lash around one rein and fastening it to keep the reins up near the horse's gullet. Thus the reins are wrapped snugly round the horse's neck. Not only is this the best way for lungeing but if the horse is being loose-schooled over fences there is no risk that the reins will catch on anything. It is far kinder to the leather than the more slapdash method of replacing the first wrap around the horse's neck with umpteen twists in the reins.

The first, correct way is very quick providing you learn the knack of how to do it. If you begin by gently pulling the reins over to the left side of the horse while turning to face in the same direction as the horse, you can then put your right arm holding the slack of the left rein nearest the buckle in your right hand and nearest the bit in your left so that it looks like a skipping-rope falling down between your two hands. Now the rein can be given a quick flip up and over (not on to) the horse's ears and the whole manoeuvre is completed within a moment.

### Boots/bandages

The horse should wear boots or bandages in order to prevent injury to his legs from interfering or hitting himself with one of his other feet.

When a young horse starts his training his natural coordination is interrupted by all the new work he is given to think about and to perform. Thus he becomes very ungainly in his movements and his extremities lack their normal control while he is busy trying to assimilate his trainer's thoughts and commands. Added to this, as yet his whole body lacks the required muscle tone. The horse's feet have very hard horn walls, which are later shod with even harder metal; it is essential to protect his legs from injuries which can prove to be permanent, e.g. large, unsightly splints. A long-striding horse should wear overreach boots . . . again, prevention is better than cure.

### A lunge-whip

This is a craftsman's tool; it should *never* be treated as an instrument of torture. The lunge-whip is a reinforcing forward-driving aid; it is an extension of the trainer's hand and arm, and in a way it is his 'legs' as well!

It is imperative to remember that the lunge-whip is an aid for the *horse* as, by its tactful use, the lunger can help the horse to improve his balance, his muscle work, his form and his action, as he works on a circle around his trainer.

A lunge-whip needs to be selected with care; it must not be so heavy that it is cumbersome. It needs to be well-balanced and yet long enough for the trainer to be able to touch the horse's trunk with the tip of the lash when the horse is trotting on a smaller-sized circle of approximately 12 m (39 ft) in diameter. All lungers should

*It is essential to protect the horse's legs from self-inflicted injuries. A long-striding horse should wear overreach boots . . . prevention is better than cure.*

understand how to use the lunge-whip correctly to help the horse's understanding and balance and to promote better muscle work. To use a lunge-whip to its fullest effect is a great art – to use a lunge-whip as a punishment for a lack of understanding is barbaric.

There may be very rare occasions – it has happened to me three times in fifty years – when a lunge-whip may be used forcefully as a means of self-protection, but even then it must *never* be aimed at the horse's head. His eyes are too vulnerable and they are irreplaceable.

*Side reins*

These should be light and long enough; they should have at least 14 holes for adjustments and should have strong, safe spring-clips or buckles at the end to fasten either on to the rings of the cavesson or, later, on to the rings of the snaffle bit.

Side reins made of plain leather are the lightest and most efficient. Those with rubber inserts weigh more and tend to swing about unless they are tightened too much, and some horses learn to 'tease' them with little leanings.

## Advantages of side reins

The use of side reins is a complex and controversial subject. As with all items of horse-training equipment, side reins must never be used for purposes of force or abuse. There are, however, several valid reasons for their use such as:

1. To assist the trainer to control strong, wayward horses; in this case, side reins

may help to channel the horse's ideas and to aid his concentration, especially when he is being worked out of doors or in strange surroundings.

2. Similarly, in the case of self-willed horses who have been spoiled in their early training, side reins can be of great assistance in helping the horse to understand that he should work honestly and willingly, forwards on the exact track that the trainer prescribes for him, without throwing his head about or trying to turn in towards his trainer or to turn right around and dash off in the other direction.

3. As a preliminary to working on long-reins and to being backed, side reins can be used for a period of a few days to encourage young horses to seek and trust a contact with the bit.

4. Spoiled horses who have lost their confidence due to an uneducated rider's bad and jostling hands may be helped to regain their trust by the feel of light side reins which stay quietly and consistently in place as they work forward at trot on the lunge.

5. If the trainer or rider is unable to ride for a while, he can maintain the muscle work and training standard of his trained horse by using side reins for the middle part of his lunge sessions to assist him with piaffe and for some work in collection at trot and canter – never at walk!

*To fit side reins*

Side reins may be fitted if required when the horse is well accustomed to working in a snaffle bridle and has accepted the feel of side reins fixed to the side rings on the front of the lungeing cavesson's noseband.

When the horse is halted the trainer and an assistant should measure the side reins while standing on each side of the horse. The trainer should ensure that they are long enough before they are clipped on simultaneously and gently, and that they are fitted so that they are reasonably slack. It is imperative that the horse does not feel trapped after both side reins are clipped on to the snaffle rings. If the trainer does not have an assistant it is important that he is doubly careful; he should fasten the outside rein first.

The trainer himself should check that the side reins are equal in length, not by counting the holes but by standing in front of the horse when he is standing squarely and evenly on all four legs. The trainer then places the first two fingers of both hands on the outer ends of the mouthpiece of the snaffle and gently pulls them forwards to make both reins taut; they should match exactly in length, height and tension when the horse is standing still.

When the pressure and effect of loose side reins have been felt and understood over a period of three or four consecutive days, the trainer and his assistant can work together at gradually shortening the side reins until they are nearly straight when the horse is halted. When the horse moves forward he flexes his muscles, thereby shortening his frame for this activity and the side reins will be loose enough for him to move freely forward.

Side reins should be adjusted to an equal length to enable the lunger to work the horse onto the outside rein while keeping a light, pliable contact through the lunge rein as if it were the inner rein; thus the inner side rein will often be a little slack.

Side reins should never be shortened so that they pull the lower part of the horse's head in towards his chest in an endeavour to force the head and neck into a set shape or outline. They should never cause discomfort.

They should be attached to the roller at a height which is level with the middle part of the horse's shoulder-blades, just below the centre point for a young horse, and above it for a more trained horse.

Well-fitted side reins should allow the horse to use and develop his musculature as well as his understanding and the quality of his gaits. They should *never* be too tight. As a guide, when working at trot and canter the horse should always be able to push his nose forward so that it is carried a hand's breadth in front of a vertical line running down the front of his face.

## Limitations of side reins

Some trainers regard side reins as a necessary part of lungeing equipment – others prefer to work their horses free although they may concede that 'side reins may be used by those trainers whose lungeing is not good enough to be effective without their use!' But it must be understood that side reins have their limitations and should be used with discretion. They may even be destructive and dangerous in certain circumstances, such as if they are introduced too early in the training programme or in the lesson period, or if they are introduced or used in a forceful rather than in an intelligent and tactful

The trainer should check that the side reins are even from the front when the horse is standing square. These reins look tight at the halt but at trot and canter they were just right.

a

b

*Improvization . . . roller and breast girth.*

*Talland Stream goes forward at canter onto the outside rein. An ex-racehorse, this was the first time he had worn a crupper.*

manner. Any horse at any time may panic due to a fear of the unyielding restriction which side reins impose upon him. He may react unexpectedly, suddenly and violently, rearing up, sometimes to the point of losing his balance or of throwing himself over backwards.

If side reins are not removed for all but the briefest periods of work at walk, the horse's walk gait may be destroyed. At walk the horse needs complete freedom of his head and neck and full use of his neck muscles and of all the many related trunk muscles in order to develop good ground-covering strides in a true walk rhythm and sequence of footfalls. If side reins are not

removed for this gait, their use may change a walk into a lateral gaited pace or amble.

Similarly side reins should always be removed for all work over ground-poles and all cavalletti and fences. Just as side reins can exchange a walk for a pace, so will they change a free jumper into a stopper, because a horse physically cannot jump if his head and his neck are put out of action.

Lungers must at all times be aware of the risks to horse, rider and trainer involved in the use of side reins and should take the following precautions:

1. Horses should never be led from their

*Talland Stream has adjusted his balance and found self-carriage – a soft and light contact.*

stables to the lunge area with the side reins clipped on to the bit. If they are frightened as they are led across a hard and/or slippery surface, there is a real risk they may panic and rear over backwards due to coming against the restriction of the side reins and the sudden pain they feel in their mouths.

2. Always unfasten the side reins and clip them up onto the D's at the top of the training roller or the saddle whenever the horse is halted for any length of time, when he is going to be worked for more than one circle at a walk, before putting up a rider and before making any adjustments to the rider or to the the horse's equipment.

3. If and when it is deemed necessary to fit side reins they must be fitted with great care and should be adjusted to suit each individual horse's needs.

4. Side reins should not be clipped on to the snaffle rings on a young horse until he is thoroughly accustomed to wearing a bridle, to working forward freely and obediently at walk and trot, and he has started to find his own natural balance and coordination when being lunged on a large circle. Every young horse should be completely confident about being lunged while wearing side reins fixed to his cavesson before the side reins are fitted on to the snaffle bit.

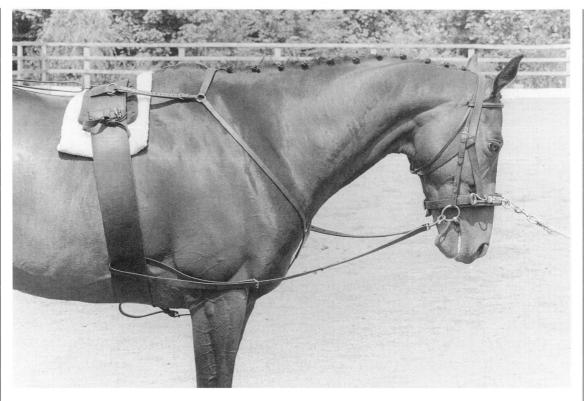

*Side reins which are fitted much too low. Talland Stream's face expresses resigned disapproval.*

5. If a more experienced horse is going to be worked in side reins they should not be clipped on to the bit until he has been worked in on the lunge, on both reins and he is warmed up and settled down.

6. It is dangerous for the lunger to regard side reins as a guaranteed method to force a horse to go on the bit and in a correct outline. If such ignorant methods are used on hot-blooded, high-couraged and sensitive horses, the lunger risks ruining all the good training he may have put into the horse up to then, and the stress and strain can cause chronic upset and lameness.

Many lightly built and highly strung Thoroughbred and Arabian horses, with dainty muzzles and narrow, fragile lower jaws, fear and resent the fixed restriction imposed by side reins. Rather than seeking a contact with the bit they will come up against it, panic and fight. Such a reaction should be met with sympathetic understanding and it should be parried with intelligence rather than a rise in temper temperature. If untold harm is to be avoided, the side reins must be abandoned at once and the horse set to work again with his head and neck free. At the end of the lesson, the young horse should be given a mouthful of long grass as a reward for good work in the last exercise; the grass will become entwined

*Side reins too tight – the horse looks like a mountain goat or an elephant on a tub. (This often happens in a dressage test when the rider makes excessive use of his hands.)*

around the bit and will have a suitable long-lasting reward effect and give a pleasurable sensation. When he is still munching, light, loose side reins should be clipped on to the bit and then the horse should be led forward quietly round the schooling area. The horse should be halted and rewarded, after which the side reins should be unfastened, put up on to the top D's or rings and the horse put away in his stable. The lunger must continue with this slow but sure method of restoring the horse's confidence for several days or even weeks.

The long grass provides a most acceptable reward as well as a most natural way of encouraging the horse to relax his lower jaw and his poll. The lunger must be generous with his praise, replenishing the grass as frequently as may be necessary and must judge when the horse's confidence has been restored sufficiently before asking for a few strides at trot.

I have cured many horses by this simple method – reasoning and kindness will succeed where brute force has failed.

7. Side reins should never be fitted too loose and too low or there will be a grave risk that the horse might put one of his front feet over one of them should he put down his head or strike out in a temper.

the left hand is the rein hand when the horse works on the left rein and the right hand is the whip hand, and vice versa. Holding and using the equipment in this way is simple; each hand has its own duty to perform, quite separately yet in unison, and there is no confusion over which hand does what duty. This is a vital factor in stressful conditions such as when lungeing badly trained, aggressive or wilful horses, and for lungeing horses over fences. Moreover, this method enables the lunger to adapt to the strongest possible holding posture in one eye-blink time (see pages 42 and 43).

The method of carrying the spare loops of lunge-rein in the whip hand is incorrect; it is very cumbersome and impedes the flow and accuracy of the whip's movement, added to which it renders it impossible to make an immediate and correct change of stance in order to control an obstreperous horse. Also incorrect is the 'figure-of-eight' method of looping the lunge-rein back and forth in the rein hand so that the hand is cluttered with a double amount of lunge-rein, coming out of the hand in all directions! If anyone should doubt the truth of this, I suggest they try these two methods when lungeing a 'sharp' young horse over a few fences!

It is imperative that you make thoughtful preparations before you start to lunge a horse. Later is often too late! You must always prepare the lunge rein as described below, so that it is coiled correctly into the rein hand with the clip end on top and the stop or 'handle' end underneath.

For their safety as well as for their education, all potential trainers and/or

assistants must be taught how to coil and hold a lunge-rein in a correct, efficient and fluent manner, with each loop containing a little less than 1 m (3 ft) of rein, all loops hanging perfectly flat, untwisted and being of even lengths without any tangles.

*To coil the lunge-rein*

If you are about to work the horse on the left rein, hold the lunge-rein 30–50 cm (1–1½ ft) from the clip or buckle attached to the horse's cavesson in your right hand and, with quick but unobtrusive arm-stretching movements with the left hand,

a

measure out about 1 m (3 ft) of rein into the right hand. Repeat this, twisting the rein to make it lie flat as you go, and put each loop on top of the previous one, until the whole length of the lunge-rein is coiled neatly into your right hand. Then transfer the coils of this rein into the left hand so that the clip-end loop of the lunge-rein is now nearest to the horse and it can be released fluently, loop by smoothly running loop, as required.

If the horse is handed over to you as the lunger with the lunge-rein in a disorganized tangle, but amid the easiest of circumstances, i.e. on a reasonably dry and clean surface, retain your hold on the rein 30–50 cm (1–1½ ft) from the horse's head, and quietly drop the spare part of the rein onto the ground. Watch the horse as you do this and reassure him with your voice. You can then disentangle the rein by quietly shaking it free before coiling it into

*To lunge on the right rein, hold the rein quite close to the horse and coil the rope in even loops into the left hand. When completed, transfer the lunge-rein into the right hand from where it will run out freely, and take the whip in the left hand. (Please note my 'helpful' lungeing partner!)*

b

c

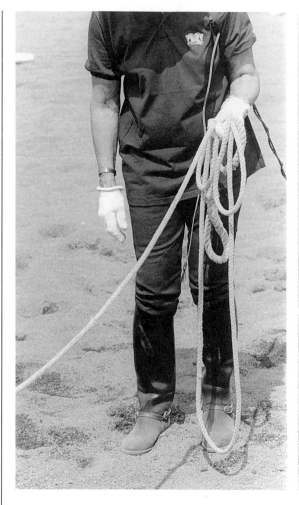 

*How NOT to hold a lunge-rein. (Please note that the author's spurs have very short necks but provide essential ankle support – my left ankle was smashed forty years ago.)*

*A figure-of-eight is too complicated if a horse really plays up and/or for lungeing over fences. NEVER put your hand into the trap of the loop.*

your right hand as described above, and finally transferring the whole of the rein into the left hand ready to lunge the horse on the left rein.

Many young horses are afraid of a rope or rein moving on the ground near to them, possibly due to an inborn fear of snakes, so this method provides an additional bonus as

a useful exercise for improving a young horse's confidence and steadiness to ropes or other objects moving around near his feet.

You have to be extremely dexterous in your handling of the rein if the surface is wet, as you must not let the rein drop into the mud. You must manage the reorganization of the rein, off the ground, between your coils into the left hand, before finally taking over the completely coiled rein.

If you place your index finger over the first coil of the lunge-rein, i.e. that which runs directly to the horse, this will divide it from the remainder of the loops, and the cross-over thus supplied within the lunger's hand gives you a more secure hold on the lunge-rein itself.

It is most important that the loops of the lunge-rein are kept exactly even and of the correct length; one over-long loop can trip up the lunger and just one loop which is short and wound round the hand can break that same hand if the horse plays up, or cause more serious injuries if the horse manages to run off, dragging the lunger behind him.

*The hold on the rein — when it is attached to the horse*

The lunger's rein hand should be held as for riding or driving with the thumb part uppermost, the base knuckles facing towards the horse and the fingers closed firmly on the rein, with the fingertips on the hand's cushion. The elbow behind the hand and the slightly rounded wrist should be kept close to the lunger's body, while the hand retains an elastic contact or allows a tiny rewarding 'give', whatever is required. There should be no stiffness or excess tension in any of the joints of the lunger's limbs.

As when riding, there should be a smooth contact between the lunger's hand and the lower part of the horse's head. This contact should not have a heavy 'dead' feel for that would have too strong and nullifying an

*If you place your index finger over the coil of the lunge-rein which runs directly to the horse, this gives a very secure hold (see page 36).*

two hands. With practice this can be accomplished in a quick and efficient manner.

The procedure is reversed in order to prepare the lunge-rein for work on the right rein, i.e. the left hand holds the cavesson end of the lunge-rein whilst the right hand measures, gathers and feeds the influence and can cause the horse to 'lock' in his poll. Instead the tension should be alive to the need of the moment. At no time should the lunge-rein be allowed to hang down in festoons on the ground between the lunger's hand and the horse's cavesson, as this clearly signifies lack of contact and deterioration of the work; further it may lead to loss of control and consequent accident and injuries.

At all times the lunger's stance should be good; always be aware of where your feet are and of what they are doing – that may sound obvious, but how often the obvious is over-looked! Good footwork, posture, poise and an instinctive awareness combine to safeguard the lunger's balance, control of the horse, body language and the effectiveness of his lungeing. The lunger's latent strength is based on a secure but mobile stance, a strong neck and back and firmly held shoulder-blades. From this firm base of shoulder-blades through to supple shoulder joints, the lunger should use the muscles which run down the back of his upper arms and along the under part of his forearms, through supple elbows, wrists,

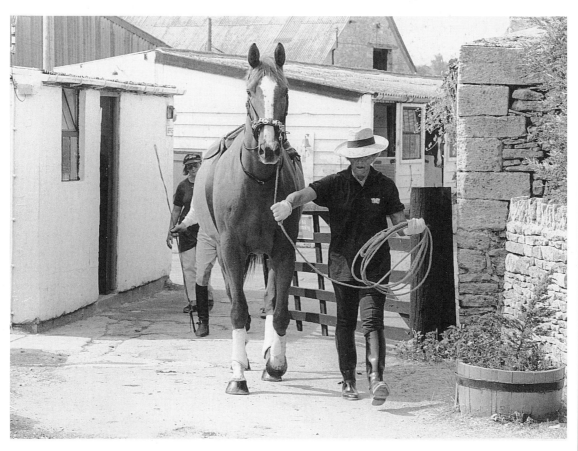

*The leader should keep the horse moving well forward, shoulder to shoulder. Here the leader adopts the strong hold and the assistant follows directly and helpfully in the rear.*

hands and base finger bones to the rein and thence to the horse's head. As with the rider, the lunger's rein aids have their beginnings in, and can call on a powerful strength from, the muscles at the back of a well-carried head and neck and the two shoulder-blades.

The lunger must be quick and firm in his mind and on his feet in order to retain the essential alignment with the horse's shoulders for restraining, and towards his hindquarters for a forward-driving influence.

*A trained and well-managed horse may be led with the hand underneath the rein.*

## Actions of the lunge-rein

The contact, with which the trainer teaches the horse to work, should always be present; it should be given and used by the lunger; it should not be developed into a dead pull by the horse. By the means of thoughtful contact the lunger is able to influence the horse, providing that the hand is sufficiently educated and is trustworthy. The lunger's rein aids act in the following ways:

1. *Leading, indicating direction.* When leading the horse in hand the leader should always keep the horse moving well forward, shoulder to shoulder. As a general rule she should hold the leading or lunge-rein in the strong position, with the back of the hand which is nearest to the horse uppermost, the thumb away from the horse, and keeping a good grip on the rein. Her hand should be on top of the rein with the fingernails facing downwards.

While remaining in command of the situation with a firm grasp on the rein, the leader should move her hand forward in time with the horse's movement to allow the horse's head and his neck and trunk muscles free play. The remainder of the lunge-rein should be correctly coiled into the hand furthest away from the horse; the outside hand also carries the whip and should be placed on the leader's left hip joint if the horse plays up. In practice the horse should be led and lunged equally to either hand.

A trained and well-mannered horse may be led with the hand underneath the rein, but the first, strong position is the safer of the two if the horse is strange to the leader or the environment, if he is undisciplined, fresh or young and untrained.

Incidentally, legally, just as a bridle is required for leading a horse on the public highway, the strong position with the back of the hand uppermost is also the one that is acceptable against a claim of negligence in controlling a led horse in a court of law.

The feeling of 'leading' should be continued when working a horse on the lunge. The rein hand should lead the horse forward, slightly in front of the bit. When the lunge-rein is attached to the front ring of the cavesson this is easy! The lunger should keep her elbow close to her upper body in order to retain a good, easy posture, to stabilize and soften her rein aids and to be able to exact an instant and strong hold should the need arise. As a general practice the lunger should turn forearm, wrist and hand so that the rein is taken forward with the fingernails slightly uppermost – in the same way as a rider would apply an opening rein when guiding a young horse.

2. *Giving.* By moving the rein hand very slightly towards the horse's muzzle when leading or lungeing, the lunger can make a tiny 'give'; this may be as a form of reward or as an endeavour to counteract stiffness or resistance in the horse's poll, or as a means to develop and test the horse's sub-mission and self-carriage. These little 'gives' should be subtle and should not disturb the horse's balance, his form or the direction of his footwork.

3. *Restraining.* The lunger turns her wrist to bring the finger knuckles of her hand towards her body, moving the lunge-rein smoothly but firmly against the horse's movement. The lunger keeps her elbow close to, or even tightly braced into her body and moves the rein hand closer in order to keep the horse on the circle track or to bring him in on a smaller circle. In the latter case the lunger must adjust the

rein loops to suit the circle on which she wishes the horse to work.

The trainer must use thoughts and voice to teach the horse to understand that distinct vibrations or 'waves' created by carefully measured vertical wrist-shakes down the lunge-rein to the horse's muzzle are commands to make a half-halt, to steady the pace of the gait in which he is working, or to make a downward transition. The lunger must learn how to create these 'waves' by giving two, three or four quick up-and-down flips with his hand and wrist. This is a

a

lunge skill which can only be perfected by conscientious practice. Horses soon learn to respond according to the degree of the 'waves' sent to them down the rein.

## Using the lunge-rein

It is most important that the lunger learns to get a correct 'feel' for using the lunge-rein with a contact which is elastic yet consistent and is also to a certain extent creative, interesting and physically improving to the horse. The lunge-rein is best attached to the centre ring of the cavesson when the cavesson is positioned where a correctly fitted drop noseband would be, i.e. four fingers' breadth above the top edge of the nostrils with the back-strap passing below

*Pupils should practise coiling the lunge-rein deftly into even loops, giving each coil a small twist so that it is flat with the fellow loop. These actions should be so well practised that they become instinctive and cause no disruption to the lunger's thought aid (see page 48).*

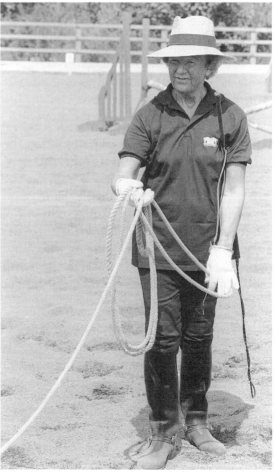

c

hand and place the knuckles of that hand on the rear part of your right hip joint; thus your right hand is anchored securely behind your stance and body-weight.

4. Reverse the whip and grasp the rein with your left hand on top of the rein and about 75 cm (2½ ft) from your right hand, to re-establish a 'feel' with the horse on the rein in a similar manner to a deep-sea fisherman, playing a fish on his line. In this procedure the left elbow should retain a slight bend; the right hand is the 'anchor' hand.

5. You must be firm and quick on your feet in order to retain the essential alignment with the horse's head.

The strength and anchorage given to the lunger by the adoption of this stance is quite remarkable; it enables comparatively small lungers to control proportionately huge horses.

## Handling the lunge-whip

The whip should be carried in the opposite hand to the rein on which the horse is working or with which he is being led. Normally it should be carried with the thong and lash furled, twined down the

*Here the lunger has been too slow to move his right foot forward towards the horse's shoulder, but he changed his position with lightning speed and controlled the horse with ease.*

your upper limb; its main use is to encourage the horse to use his trunk muscles better when moving forward over the ground. A lunge-whip should hardly ever be used as a punishment; it should not be used in front of the horse's shoulder and should *never* be used in temper.

It is important from the start to develop an adept technique with the whip hand so that it does not have to be thought about; its action should be trained to be instant, instinctive and wise.

When the horse is working, the lunger should use the whip hand to keep the whip moving quietly and rhythmically up, forward, down and around with a circling action which seems to imply, 'Keep going forward . . . better!'

Should the horse need a little extra encouragement the lunger may wish to emphasize the point with a little 'sting-hit'. The accuracy of this work is best practised using an inanimate object such as a New Zealand rug draped over a saddle-horse, until the instructor is satisfied with the lunger's accuracy, and is confident that he or she can use the whip to touch the rug exactly how and where he wishes.

The aim should be to train the horse to come to a square halt out on the circle track when he sees the lunger raise the whip to an upright position. Most horses learn to respond to the signal with alacrity and pride! When the whip is upright it is very easy for the lunger to furl the thong down and around the stock by several quick-fingered turns of the stock itself, prior to tucking the whip under the rein-hand arm or exchanging it deftly behind his back if he is about to change the rein.

It is very important that learner-lungers are warned of the threatening effect of a lunge-whip; *never* approach any horse or pony with the lunge-whip held in the first position, i.e. active/attentive. This rule is most important if the horse and the lunger are strangers to each other, as unfortunately many horses have suffered cruel punishment from a long whip.

Lungers must always be clear, fair, firm and generous with their reward for work well done. Reward may be given in the form of a word of praise, a pat or a titbit.

## Practice techniques

There are many techniques to be learned in connection with handling the horse and lungeing equipment, each one of which must be perfected before a learner-lunger can pass the test and be entrusted with the responsible task of lungeing a horse on his or her own. Besides being valuable in a commercial or mercenary sense, horses are sensitive, vulnerable creatures, so that a few mistakes on the part of the lunger can cause mental or physical injury to the horse which, if stressed, may be irreparable.

Would-be lungers should get together to practise each technique separately before putting the different parts together:

1. They can practise coiling the lunge-rein deftly and quickly into even loops which are of a suitable length for the lunger (40–50 cm from the top [approximately 1½ ft] to the bottom of the loop is a useful average for a short lunger). They should learn the knack of giving each coil a small twist so that it lies flat against its fellow loops in and from the lunger's hand.

*The whip should be introduced to the horse with extreme care. If the trainer is calm, kind and reassuring, the horse's apprehension will soon be replaced by confidence.*

stock and secured. When working a horse on the lunge, the whip is usually carried with the thong and lash hanging free, ready to effect better muscle use within the horse's body.

Tact is a quality required for correct whip use; whilst it should stimulate better movement it should *never* create excess tension in the horse's mind or in his body.

The whip should be introduced to the horse with prudence and consideration. It should be furled at rest and then rubbed gently over the main muscle areas of the

horse's neck, trunk and hindquarters. The horse should be rewarded for standing still.

The lunger must always be vigilant and take great care that his lunge-whip never causes upset to any other horses that are working nearby.

### The four basic whip positions

1. Attentive/active. The whip is held with the point uppermost and towards the horse, the thong and lash twirling softly and

*The lunger's whip should retain an 'alive' look as it is circled up, forward and round. It should not be passive with the tip wearing out on the ground.*

*The whip furled and reversed.*

*Furling the whip when working a whip-sl*

rhythmically in a clockwise or anti-clockwise direction, in time with the horse as he works on the right or left rein. If the point is aimed towards his shoulders this will push the horse out on to the big circle track; if the point is directed towards his hindquarters the inference will be for more impulsion.

2. At rest. Without changing your hold on the whip stock, move the point of the whip back, away from the horse, until the whip lies along the top of your forearm with the point and thong behind you.

3. Reversed. The whip itself is reversed and held upside-down with the point behind the lunger and pointing down towards, but not on, the ground, virtually out of sight from the horse.

4. Furled and reversed and at the ready to lead the horse in hand or to walk up to him. As long as the horse is not at all nervous of the whip, the quickest way to furl a lunge-whip is to raise the tip and hold the whip vertical to the ground; then, by quick turning of the stock, the lash is curled evenly down the stock and may be tied with one simple knot round it, near the bottom. If the horse is whip-shy, you will have to use a more discreet method of winding the lash around the stock, while holding the whip in a lower position, until you have gained the horse's confidence.

If you wish to approach the horse from the centre of the lungeing area or require the use of both hands to reward the horse or to adjust the tack, furl the whip and then tuck it high up under your arm with the point down behind you; never leave the whip on the ground where horses might tread on and break it.

## The use of the whip

The lunge-whip should always be with thoughtful and controlled mov It should never be waved about wit ingless gesticulations – it must be us the utmost skill, tact, and care. The whip should be used with discretion a minimum degree so that the horse calm, attentive and willing. Every that is made with the whip should purpose and meaning which the learns to understand and respect.

Look at the lunge-whip as an extens

*The whip should not be passive, with the thong and lash like the line of a fishing rod before a bite. Practice is necessary, especially when learning how to touch up a lazy horse with a sting-hit on his hindquarters.*

2. They should practise with a lunge-rein tied to a post until they can pay it out or take it up, as required, both quickly and smoothly, the left hand helping the right hand and vice versa.

3. They should learn how to handle the lunge-whip. A horse rug draped over a wall, a saddle-horse or a stable door makes quite a useful horse substitute on which they can learn how to place and feel the effects of the whip lash.

4. Next, to improve their skills, would-be lungers should practise the correct handling of the rein and whip with a mobile assistant; it is helpful to do this with a friend, working in pairs, until they have developed a reliable dexterity which should be tested by an experienced lunger before they risk working a live (and lively!) horse or pony.

---

## SAFETY WARNINGS

◆ Avoid putting your hand into the 'trap' of the loop at the end of the lunge-rein.

◆ Beware of shortening or tightening the coils – keep a constant watch on the size of the loops of the spare part of the rein; *none* of these must ever be allowed to sneak into a smaller size than 35 cm (1 ft) from the heel of the hand, or the hand could be trapped; one or more long loops can form dangerous foot traps!

◆ Remember that great care must be taken when approaching a horse with a lunge-whip and when changing the whip from one hand to the other as, instinctively, often reinforced by recall of abuse in the past, most horses are wary of a lunge-whip.

*The whip should be introduced to the horse with extreme care. If the trainer is calm, kind and reassuring, the horse's apprehension will soon be replaced by confidence.*

stock and secured. When working a horse on the lunge, the whip is usually carried with the thong and lash hanging free, ready to effect better muscle use within the horse's body.

Tact is a quality required for correct whip use; whilst it should stimulate better movement it should *never* create excess tension in the horse's mind or in his body.

The whip should be introduced to the horse with prudence and consideration. It should be furled at rest and then rubbed gently over the main muscle areas of the

horse's neck, trunk and hindquarters. The horse should be rewarded for standing still.

The lunger must always be vigilant and take great care that his lunge-whip never causes upset to any other horses that are working nearby.

### The four basic whip positions

1. Attentive/active. The whip is held with the point uppermost and towards the horse, the thong and lash twirling softly and

*The lunger's whip should retain an 'alive' look as it is circled up, forward and round. It should not be passive with the tip wearing out on the ground.*

rhythmically in a clockwise or anti-clockwise direction, in time with the horse as he works on the right or left rein. If the point is aimed towards his shoulders this will push the horse out on to the big circle track; if the point is directed towards his hindquarters the inference will be for more impulsion.

2. At rest. Without changing your hold on the whip stock, move the point of the whip back, away from the horse, until the whip lies along the top of your forearm with the point and thong behind you.

3. Reversed. The whip itself is reversed and held upside-down with the point behind the lunger and pointing down towards, but not on, the ground, virtually out of sight from the horse.

4. Furled and reversed and at the ready to lead the horse in hand or to walk up to him. As long as the horse is not at all nervous of the whip, the quickest way to furl a lunge-whip is to raise the tip and hold the whip vertical to the ground; then, by quick turning of the stock, the lash is curled evenly down the stock and may be tied with one simple knot round it, near

*The whip furled and reversed.*

*Furling the whip when working a whip-shy horse.*

the bottom. If the horse is whip-shy, you will have to use a more discreet method of winding the lash around the stock, while holding the whip in a lower position, until you have gained the horse's confidence.

If you wish to approach the horse from the centre of the lungeing area or require the use of both hands to reward the horse or to adjust the tack, furl the whip and then tuck it high up under your arm with the point down behind you; never leave the whip on the ground where horses might tread on and break it.

## The use of the whip

The lunge-whip should always be handled with thoughtful and controlled movements. It should never be waved about with meaningless gesticulations – it must be used with the utmost skill, tact, and care. The lunge-whip should be used with discretion and to a minimum degree so that the horse remains calm, attentive and willing. Every gesture that is made with the whip should convey purpose and meaning which the horse learns to understand and respect.

Look at the lunge-whip as an extension of

your upper limb; its main use is to encourage the horse to use his trunk muscles better when moving forward over the ground. A lunge-whip should hardly ever be used as a punishment; it should not be used in front of the horse's shoulder and should *never* be used in temper.

It is important from the start to develop an adept technique with the whip hand so that it does not have to be thought about; its action should be trained to be instant, instinctive and wise.

When the horse is working, the lunger should use the whip hand to keep the whip moving quietly and rhythmically up, forward, down and around with a circling action which seems to imply, 'Keep going forward . . . better!'

Should the horse need a little extra encouragement the lunger may wish to emphasize the point with a little 'sting-hit'. The accuracy of this work is best practised using an inanimate object such as a New Zealand rug draped over a saddle-horse, until the instructor is satisfied with the lunger's accuracy, and is confident that he or she can use the whip to touch the rug exactly how and where he wishes.

The aim should be to train the horse to come to a square halt out on the circle track when he sees the lunger raise the whip to an upright position. Most horses learn to respond to the signal with alacrity and pride! When the whip is upright it is very easy for the lunger to furl the thong down and around the stock by several quick-fingered turns of the stock itself, prior to tucking the whip under the rein-hand arm or exchanging it deftly behind his back if he is about to change the rein.

It is very important that learner-lungers are warned of the threatening effect of a lunge-whip; *never* approach any horse or pony with the lunge-whip held in the first position, i.e. active/attentive. This rule is most important if the horse and the lunger are strangers to each other, as unfortunately many horses have suffered cruel punishment from a long whip.

Lungers must always be clear, fair, firm and generous with their reward for work well done. Reward may be given in the form of a word of praise, a pat or a titbit.

## Practice techniques

There are many techniques to be learned in connection with handling the horse and lungeing equipment, each one of which must be perfected before a learner-lunger can pass the test and be entrusted with the responsible task of lungeing a horse on his or her own. Besides being valuable in a commercial or mercenary sense, horses are sensitive, vulnerable creatures, so that a few mistakes on the part of the lunger can cause mental or physical injury to the horse which, if stressed, may be irreparable.

Would-be lungers should get together to practise each technique separately before putting the different parts together:

1. They can practise coiling the lunge-rein deftly and quickly into even loops which are of a suitable length for the lunger (40–50 cm from the top [approximately 1½ ft] to the bottom of the loop is a useful average for a short lunger). They should learn the knack of giving each coil a small twist so that it lies flat against its fellow loops in and from the lunger's hand.

# 5

# *Understanding and Harmonizing the Natural Aids*

## GENERAL PRINCIPLES

It is always a false economy to attempt to train a young horse unless you yourself have been well trained and unless you have gained plenty of practical experience with trained horses and mischievous ponies whilst being guided and supervised by an experienced instructor.

Part of every lunger's training should be spent watching good trainers working horses on the lunge. If you are permitted to observe such demonstrations they are invaluable. It is so important that trainers are far-sighted and generous, and that they encourage young people to watch their training sessions whenever possible, so that safe and classical methods are preserved for future generations of horse trainers.

A good trainer will always make a point of creating a strong link-up between the horse's brain and his own brain before he embarks on each and every work session; he will also make sure that this vital link-up is kept safe and secure throughout each lesson. The quality of the rapport between the trainer and the horse is of the utmost importance to the success of every horse's training.

A good trainer will make always full use of spontaneous reward throughout every horse's training.

Providing that the horse understands the trainer's request, nearly every horse has a willingness to obey, founded on a strong urge to please his trainer or rider, and an incredibly forgiving nature. However, maybe due to the tempo at which modern-day life is lived, we have changed from Xenophon's system of horse training in 400 BC, which was mainly founded on reward, to a modern system which seems to be centred around a lack of patience and understanding, shouted curses and abuse of the whip. This is a very retrograde change – not only is it unfair to the animal but also the result is not nearly so good due to the excess tension that unfair demands and incomprehensible use of the whip creates in the horse.

I believe that, as trainers, we must make space in our hearts, brains and time schedules for the excellent directive from the old British Cavalry Manual, 'Make much of your horses'. We cannot afford to lose our ability to develop a rapport with our horses.

Good trainers will be aware at all times that every move they make will be observed closely by the young horse, who is now at one of the most vulnerable and one of the most receptive stages of his career as a riding horse.

Only as a result of his or her own initial training combined with a lengthy period of handling and riding many different sorts and sizes of ponies and horses, can a learner-lunger acquire sufficient amounts of knowledge and experience to start on a career as a trainer. The training of young horses should never be embarked on lightly; not only is it full of risks to the trainer himself but also, if it is done badly, the horses will suffer and their whole lives may be blighted due to the unqualified, so-called trainer's bungling mistakes.

The trainer should ensure that everything is done to make the process of training a riding horse or pony a thoroughly natural, easy and enjoyable occurrence from the horse's point of view. In order that they may do this, trainers have to have constant recall of all the many subjects they learned in their own early lessons when they were learning to ride, and the many techniques they were taught thereafter.

It is interesting to note how the general awareness and acceptance of some seemingly complicated subjects has increased within recent years. When, as Chairman of the B.H.S. Examinations Committee, I first mentioned the need for instructors and riders to study the horse's psychology, anatomy and physiology, the majority of the examiners and instructors present looked extremely shocked and intimated that I should learn to live in the real world. Now these subjects are regarded as not only interesting but necessary. Today, these subjects are included in everyday school and college curriculums, and so fear of the unknown has been replaced by a general acceptance and understanding. A good instructor will teach his pupil at least the basic facts of why horses behave as they do, whether that's well or badly from a human point of view. One does not have to look very far to find the main factors which cause horses to think and react as they do.

## THE NATURE OF THE HORSE

Over the ages, the horse as a species has survived due to his natural instincts of self-preservation in the wild.

The horse's ancestors were creatures who lived in a herd roaming over the plains. The stallions were responsible for the protection and leadership of the herd. They were a relatively shy and peaceful species whose teeth were so formed that they could graze off every little piece of the shortest of grasses and, due to the muscular 'sling' mechanism by which their trunks were suspended between their forelegs, they were able to reach the water of quite low-lying streams, without going down on their knees – thus they could remain ready for flight.

These creatures of the plain rarely jumped and were wary of snakes (to a young horse a rope lying on the ground can look so like a snake). With the advent of Man upon the scene, horses learned to be extremely suspicious of anything which might be a trap. Many native ponies retain an instinctive fear of being shut in, even if the loose box does have a good deep bed in it.

Sharing the horses' territory on the plains were many wily, fast, savage and hungry predators, such as wolves; bolting was the main form of self-protection from these predators.

If cornered in the comparative safety of the herd, wild horses will form a tight-knit circle, with their heads inwards and their hindquarters to the outside, from whence they can lash out backwards or sideways at the enemy with one or both hind limbs.

If the attack comes from the front, horses will bite or strike out with one or both forelimbs in self-protection.

If a wild cat or similar animal with evil intent and a hearty appetite leaped onto a horse's back, his ancestors were quick to develop two most effective ways of saving their lives. The first was to leap in the air with violent kicks (bucks) to dislodge the attacker, kicking him as he fell to the ground; the second method was to squash or knock off the enemy against nearby trees or rocks.

All of these survival techniques have remained with the horse to the present day and if horses are forced into moments of panic or discomfort by their trainers or riders, domesticated horses will still resort to exactly the same defensive behaviour.

The pecking order, a term which is in general use in the countryside, is very much the rule of the herd amongst wild horses, and remains just as strong an instinct when they are turned out in the home paddock. It is usually quite easy to see which horse is the boss! It is for this reason that inexperienced people have to be warned against putting a strange horse out in a field with an already established group; he may be used to being 'top cat' in

the group he has left and will have to be put into his place by all the other horses of the new group. They will imagine he should be a junior member whereas he will consider himself to be the 'king'! Horses can be very severely injured if this fact is not borne in mind.

The majority of young horses have a natural tendency to give their carer or their trainer similar treatment to that which they mete out to companion horses in the field. It must be appreciated that it is natural for young horses to use their teeth or heels freely on the human substitute companion, in order to get their own way or to stop the human interfering or causing them harm.

Comprehension of these few facts will help would-be trainers to understand that young horses who bite, kick, rear, buck or bolt are truly overcome by their natural instincts; these horses have to be trained to behave in a more civilized manner, which they will do with fair reprimand for rude behaviour and reward for compliance. Soon they will develop into well-mannered horses as their confidence is won and developed by their educated and understanding trainers. I believe that no horse is actually born bad, but he may well be made so by humans.

It must be remembered that even the most civilized of horses can hear, see and smell a strange object well before their human counterparts can do so, as their senses of taste and touch are extremely sensitive and they are amazingly receptive to telepathic output. With thought and practice it becomes quite easy to read a horse's thoughts and moods through the many variations of his facial expressions as well as by interpreting his body language.

In his natural state the horse keeps his balance instinctively – he rarely falls over. During this time his head and neck form the balancing pole which he uses to compensate and to re-adjust when his balance becomes precarious. In the rear portion of his brain he has a wonderful mechanism which assists him to keep his balance. The cells in this area combine with gravity-power to cause immediate adaptations to coordination for balance throughout his body. Knowing this, it is easy to understand that any restriction on the horse's head carriage can change the firing pattern of these cells; consequently young horses must be allowed to have sufficient freedom of their heads and necks as they learn to balance themselves in the new work, on the lunge and when ridden.

## HARMONIZING THE NATURAL AIDS

Practice, combined with the experience of lungeing many, many horses and ponies, will develop the lunger's ability to use his or her natural aids in harmony, to produce the following effects:

*Forward driving*

1. The lunger's thoughts. These are the major influence.

2. Voice. Used with clear and meaningful intonations.

3. Body language. Fine nuances of the lunger's positioning and movement – the strongest is a deliberate forward step.

4. Tongue-clicking. An occasional click will produce an immediate reaction, unless the horse has become bored by continuous clicking to which he no longer listens.

5. The whip. Used as an extension of the lunger's arm to stimulate muscle action and to back-up the above forward-driving aids, by its movement rather than by actual contact.

The aim of this combination of the natural aids is to keep the horse thinking and working forward confidently and happily whilst building and maintaining a correct form. These aids should be used effectively but not too strongly. The horse must never be hurried out of his balance and rhythm in any of the three gaits; he can only work well if he is *confident* and *calm*.

If a horse is disinterested, lazy or even stubborn, he should receive a very quick, small, well-timed and well placed sting-hit on his hindquarters from the lash of the whip; this needs to be delivered with dexterity so that the horse feels it unmistakably but wonders from whence it came! These sting-hits should be used very sparingly as the horse needs to learn to go forward yet nothing must damage his confidence and trust.

*Restraining*

1. The lunger's thoughts. Again the most important influence.

2. Voice. Should be used at a low pitch to call the horse to attention, e.g. 'Steady' to slow down or to make a downward transition, used in conjunction with the name of the new gait. The sincerity and whole-

heartedness of the message is very important for the horse's understanding.

3. The lunger makes one or two definite 'shakes' on the lunge-rein. The horse has been taught that this disturbance on the cavesson means 'Slow down' or 'Stop'.

4. Body language. The positioning or movement of the lunger himself e.g., he may increase the distance between the horse and himself (this is invariably successful with a lazy horse); he may step towards the wall or enclosing fence or hedge before the horse approaches it, thus making good use of the wall or enclosing fence for clarity of understanding; he may make a definite step to the side towards which the horse is working (this movement can be reinforced if necessary if the lunger quickly takes the rein in his whip hand and raises his freed hand in a pedestrian 'stop' sign; he may move to head the horse straight into the perimeter fence or wall.

As soon as a halt has been achieved, the lunger must be generous and quick to *reward* the horse as he stands quite still.

*Sideways moving*

1. The lunger's thoughts. Although he wishes the horse to go sideways, 'Forwards and over, in good form' should be the image which is in the lunger's mind as the main objective.

2. Body language. The positioning or movement of the lunger – if the lunger moves towards the horse's body concentrating on the area just in front of the girth (the 'magic spot'), this will often have sufficient effect to move the horse out, forwards

and sideways, enlarging the circle in the form of leg yielding.

3. Voice. Used to translate the thoughts and coordinate them with the movement. The lunger says 'Forward and over' with an additional tongue-click as may be necessary to improve the horse's impulsion and form.

4. The whip. The tip of the whip, with the thong and lash furled, may be used on the 'magic spot' to make the thought aid more physical.

## LEARNING LUNGEING TECHNIQUES

The best way to learn to lunge, having mastered the techniques of handling the equipment, is to practise with a friend and a steady horse who is accustomed to the work, taking it in turns to lunge and be lunged while riding, with the emphasis at this stage on the horse. If one partner does not wish to be lunged he can be very helpful as an observer, watching the horse's reactions and action from the side.

*General principles*

To move the horse forward at the start of the lesson, or after changing the rein, the lunger should keep the horse on a comparatively short rein to ensure that communication is strong and control is absolute. It is so important that this stage is carried out in an exact, thoughtful and confident manner. The horse should never rush off – this is a sure indication of bad handling and training.

When he or she is lungeing a horse, the lunger forms the apex of a triangle of

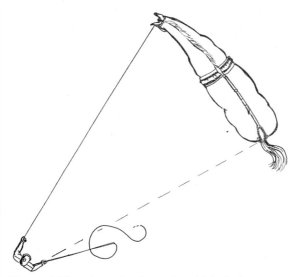

Figure 1 *The triangular frame in which the horse is worked on the lunge.*

When working a horse on a circle, the lunger should preserve a good posture as he moves his feet nearly on the spot in the centre of the circle. If he is lungeing to the left he should keep his right shoulder, hip and foot moving forward with the horse. He should urge the horse forwards on as large a circle as possible, both for his control and for the creation of a good form in the horse.

Whenever the horse is working forward at trot, the size of the circle should be about 18 m (59 ft) in diameter. Smaller circles put all the horse's joints under unnecessary strain. Until they are trained and have developed their muscles sufficiently horses should not be asked to work on circles which are less than 12 m (39 ft) in diameter.

which the horse is the base; the lunge-rein forms the line from the apex to the front of the horse and the whip forms the line from the apex to the rear of the horse (see also the photograph on page 46).

When a young horse is first learning what is expected of him when he is lunged, as opposed to being led in hand, he will be all

a

b

at sea. The trainer, who will need an assistant at this point, will have to be very active on his feet, walking on a small circle track adjacent to the assistant in this first introductory stage, and on a slightly smaller circle adjacent to the horse for the next part of the introductory stage, when the assistant has changed to a position on the outside of the horse. All of this early work is carried out at walk with frequent transitions to halt, when the horse should be rewarded immediately and generously.

Later when the horse is capable of being worked on his own on a true large circle at walk and trot and perhaps a little at canter, the trainer should stay on the spot while he encourages the horse to work on an exact circle around him as prescribed by the lunge-rein. Training the young horse to lunge is fully described in Chapter 7.

Some instructors teach their pupils to dig their inside heel into the ground and to pivot round on it. Personally, I find that concept too static; I prefer to teach that whenever the lunger works his horse on a true circle his feet should stay within the confines of 'a little dish' – as should a horse's hind feet when he performs a canter pirouette.

The consistent accuracy of the circle is important for several reasons. Although we always consider that, when a horse works on a straight or a curved line he works on a single track, he does in fact make two lines

*Three trainers demonstrate how the aids should be harmonized to help the horse to understand his lessons.*

*a  Talland Copper Cloud is given time to work out how to negotiate a new sort of eventing fence.*
*b  Talland Cavalier learns to improve his balance and the quality of his gaits on long-reins.*
*c  Talland Calendo begins to understand that piaffe just might be easier than he imagined.*

c

of hoofprints which are parallel on straight lines and which have an outer and an inner track when he works on a curved line. It is the latter factor which interests us at the moment – the curved line.

On a circle, the horse works the inner side of his body in a slightly different way from his outer side as the outer legs have further to travel and the inner legs have a little more weight to carry. These subtle differences cause the horse to work and develop his adductor and abductor muscles, to adjust his balance, to bend a little, to improve the suppleness of the whole of his body and the dexterity of his footwork. As long as the horse is lunged on a perfect circle, with his hind feet following exactly in the tracks of his fore feet, he will gain confidence in his own ability as an equine athlete and will be able to maintain his balance and regular rhythm. As a result, he will develop an improved cadence and quality into his trot gait. It is important that the lunger seeks and retains a slow yet animated rhythm which exactly suits the horse's natural balance and coordination.

*To change the rein*

The simplest way to change the rein is to halt the horse on the outer track of the circle, where he should have been taught from the first stage of his early training to stand with confident immobility. The trainer then walks up to the horse, re-coiling his rein in even loops into his other hand (as described on pages 34–7) and talking to him as he approaches, with the whip put out of action, reversed under his upper arm.

The lunger rewards the horse and teaches him how to turn on the forehand, moving his hindquarters in an arc inwards on the circle, helping him to lift the front of his trunk and arch his back so that he is able to cross his inside hindleg over in front of his outer one. The lunger may need to use the butt end of his whip softly on the 'magic spot', a hand's span above the horse's elbow, to help the horse to understand these deeper reactions and to enable him to make the turn with animation and ease.

## REMINDERS

◆ Do keep thinking like a horse. Try to analyse how he is feeling and reacting to all the work you are asking him to perform. Ask yourself 'Have I made it interesting for him?' 'Is he getting puffed?', 'Does he really understand?', 'Is his poll relaxed?', 'Is he working in a good form?', 'Have I stretched and worked the muscles equally on both sides of his body just enough to develop them, yet not enough to strain them?' Do create a mental bond between the horse and yourself.

◆ Do introduce each new piece of equipment for the horse to sniff and inspect before it is put on to him.

◆ Do, when working with a young horse, make sure that you are in a safe place, with enough space – but not too much – for the activity being addressed. A corner of a small field is a possibility, but hazards and distractions are more likely in that environment than they would be in an enclosed lungeing area or school.

◆ Do make sure that the horse is thoroughly confident about being handled, groomed and led about to either hand, to build up his trust and confidence in the midst of strange sights and sounds.

◆ Do watch the horse's attitude to each new step and sometimes even the old ones, as the young horse may have to have a 're-think' about something you assumed he has understood and accepted before he had done so.

◆ Do remember the value of working the young horse in the gait of walk when his muscles are soft and weak and his brain seems slow while he is learning so many details of what is to him an entirely new – and peculiar – facet of his life.

◆ Do remember no side reins at walk, unless you want to teach him to pace!

◆ Do feel for the horse's balance. In your desire for impulsion, do not push him out of his rhythm; allow the horse time in trot to use the ground as if it were a trampoline, rather than a running-track.

◆ Do reward generously, whenever it is earned, by praise and titbits.

◆ Do work at your technique and develop your prowess at lungeing until it reaches an art form, producing most rewarding results.

◆ Do make all lunge lessons interesting and stimulating – for yourself and your horse.

◆ Do remember that to work is an alien activity for every young horse. Physically they will be soft, flabby and weak, and mentally there is as yet no programme formatted under that heading in his brain; it is all too easy for inexperienced trainers to assume the horse understands when he does not. The young horse has to learn to work and he will do so relatively quickly if the learning process is a pleasurable experience.

◆ Do encourage others to follow your good example when you refer to 'starting to train your young horse', rather than 'breaking him in'. It is hard to think of a more barbaric and out-dated term than the latter and yet thoughtful people still use it.

◆ Do get to know and understand his mind and all that he is thinking about. Encourage him to look upon you as a fair friend from whom he has nothing to fear, a friend he can trust and upon whom he can rely.

◆ Do think quickly, act calmly and with assurance.

◆ Do be quiet, gentle and firm.

◆ Do remember to have a reward at hand and to give it to the horse whenever he has pleased you.

◆ Do remember to give instant and fair reprimand as and when needed to improve the young horse's manners, just as his mother would have done had he not been weaned. It is dangerous to allow a colt to get away with giving you a playful bite as the next one may be twice as hard. A biting colt needs a sharp slap on his muzzle and a low growl of 'Don't do that'. This may well be followed after a minute or two by a friendly pat and stroke of his muzzle so that he understands that, as long as he does not bite, you still love him a lot.

◆ Do develop an astute sense of timing.

## WARNINGS

◆ Do not move about or introduce new things to the horse in a diffident or hesitant manner as this will always arouse his suspicions, and make him nervy and jumpy.

◆ Do not ever lose your temper with a young horse. If there is an upset, trainers should count to at least a hundred and then look for the logical reason for it; a trainer must be ready to admit the fault was his and not that of the horse.

◆ Do not tie the horse up like an oven-ready chicken, with too-tight side reins or with innumerable gadgets. This major error will ruin the horse's form, his musculature and his gaits and will lose you your reputation as a trainer. Remember, gadgets are only necessary if your lungeing is not good enough!

◆ Do not drive the horse forward too fast, forcing him out of his balance and rhythm.

◆ Do not punish your horse for your own ineptitude.

◆ Never overtax him, mentally or physically.

# 6

# Understanding the Horse's Physique

This chapter is included in response to the many requests, from both young and not-so-young horsemen and women, for information to enable them to gain a better understanding of the horse's conformation; what to look for and which, among the hundreds of bones and even more hundreds of muscles, are the ones they can work on with their lungeing skills to improve the horse's form and his well-being.

The quality of a lunger's work will be much enhanced by repeated research and study, understanding, and practical use of the knowledge gained. But time for research is always limited so I have tried to summarize some of the essential facts which will help a safe and reasonably proficient lunger to become an artist in the craft. There are numerous veterinary text books which contain many hundreds of pages in which the horse's anatomy and physiology are described in meticulous detail, and which are excellent for further research should a student's interest so lead him.

## DISTRIBUTION OF THE HORSE'S BODY-WEIGHT

If a horse were divided transversely through his centre, his front half would weight nearly two-thirds of his total body-weight, and his rear half would weigh approximately one-third. With the addition of a saddle, and then a rider, the front end is made heavier and heavier, and yet the poor horse gets reproached (or worse) most unfairly, for being on his forehand and clumsy.

One has to wonder how the ridden horse is supposed to correct this situation by himself, without any help from his rider. This sad yet common state of affairs can be resolved by the trainer and rider understanding that they must exert their brains and muscles in order to develop the young horse's confidence and his muscular strength, his balance and his form by good training and correct daily work.

When the horse wanders free over the plain, cropping the grass short as he goes, his muscles are used mostly to eat the grass, to roam seeking pastures new, mainly at walk, to drink from streams, to lie down and get up again. Wild horses seldom look in the good condition in which we like to see our riding horses. In the wild, horses rarely have to trot and gallop about, and even more rarely will they jump, unless predators or helicopters with evil intent are about. Riding horses have to carry a rider on their structurally weak backs and this is where the skill of the trainer plays such a vital part.

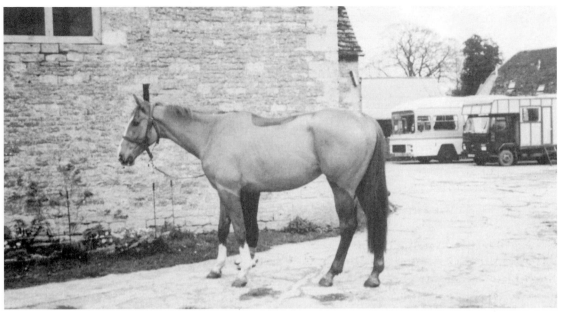

*Talland Cavalier when rising five. Already he had been in four racing stables and tried out on the flat.*

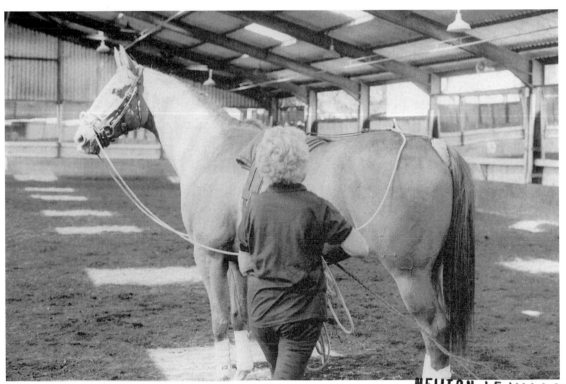

*The same horse after eighteen months of correct and thoughtful schooling.*

For the horse, his long and heavy skull works rather like a pendulum or counter-weight on the front end of the trunk muscles, which need to be developed in order that the horse may carry a rider on his back and move under him in an athletic and artistic manner. The long muscles which are inserted into the skull at the poll area or on to the tongue bone and which then stretch to the breast bone (sternum), the front of the rib-cage (thorax) or the bones of the shoulder (scapula and arm), can be used to help the horse to lift the front of his trunk so that his withers come up between his shoulder-blades, and his sternum is raised up further above his elbows. This improves the horse's posture, lightens his forehand, gives greater freedom of movement to his shoulders and provides room for the hind feet to come forward underneath the mass of the combined body-weight of the horse and rider partnership.

The lack of any skeletal attachment of the horse's fore limbs to his trunk – the horse has no collar bones – is a weakness of the riding horse's physique which should be

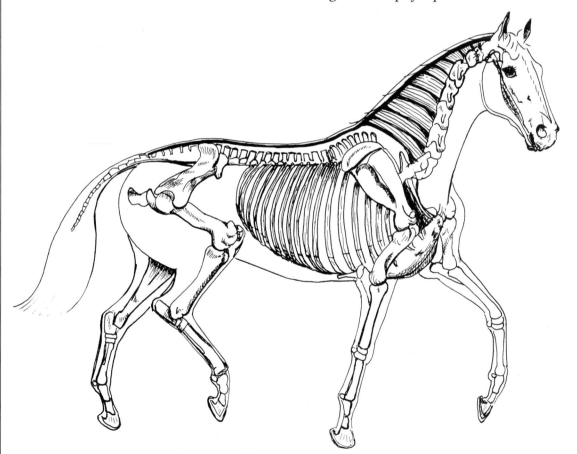

Figure 2 *The bones. The skeletal frame that lies underneath the many layers of muscle, the skin and the glossy coat.*

appreciated by trainers and riders alike. It should provide an incentive to create exercises to develop the muscle-sling which lies between the horse's shoulder-blades and in which the front of his trunk is suspended and, at the same time, to develop the muscles of his trunk and his haunches. It is well worth taking photographs of a young horse before and during his training. It will be most educational to compare the earlier photographs of the front view of the horse with photographs taken later from the same viewpoint. It is quite amazing how much the volume of all these muscles can be developed, so that a year or two later, a weak youngster whose fore limbs seem to 'come out of the same hole', and who are 'split up behind', will appear to resemble an equine Mr Atlas! Correct work will have given a 'weed' the ability to become an international 'star', as we have proved with many horses at Talland.

'Too many riders try to get activity and engagement in the hindlegs before they have helped the horse to be able to lift the front of his trunk up to leave room for his hindlegs to come forward to carry his own and his rider's body-weight.' (Boltenstern – Swedish Olympic medallist and top trainer.) Gradually (by correct work, the front of the horse, his forehand), i.e. every part of the horse's body which is in front of the rider, is raised and lightened; his back becomes stronger, with a lengthened top line and a rounded rather than a hollow feel and appearance. It is then that the horse learns to lower his croup and bring more of his weight further back on to his increasingly powerful haunches.

Although this re-adjustment of the horse's balance takes many months and even years to achieve, the goal needs to be present in the trainer's and rider's minds from the very early days of the horse's lungeing and riding career. Needless to say the work must be tactful, encouraging yet progressive. The work must be presented so that it is readily understood by the horse and generously rewarded by the trainer whenever the horse shows an improvement in his balance, connection and movement.

## THE SKELETON

The skeleton provides the foundations for the horse's form. It provides the shape, the support, and protection for all the vital internal organs, as well as the muscle attachments and leverages necessary for posture, carrying power and for movement. As no building will stand unless the foundations are good, that is the place to start. The skeleton, consisting of approximately 200 bones, is divided into two main parts:

- *The axial skeleton* is the name given to the horse's spine and the bones immediately connected to it.

- *The appendicular skeleton* is the name given to the horse's fore and hind limbs collectively.

### The axial skeleton – head to tail

*The skull*

Even the fine skull of a well-bred horse is disproportionately heavy compared with the rest of the body. The skull has to accommodate the brain as well as many

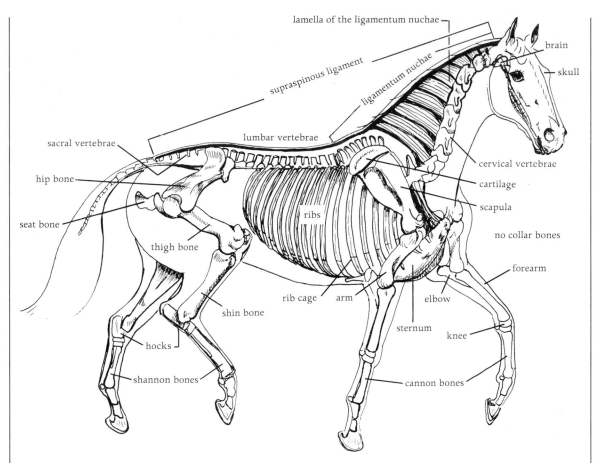

Figure 3 *The supraspinous ligament is shown as a black line, stretching from poll to tail along the horse's 'top-line'. The front portion, from poll to withers, is the ligamentum nuchae with its elastic 'fronds'.*

outsize teeth within massive jaws, together with all the ligaments and muscles which work the tongue, jaws, eyes and ears.

The horse's skull has yet another, more obscure but nevertheless major use, in that at its base, by the nape of his neck or poll, it provides secure anchorages or attachments for many of the main trunk muscles and their near relations, as will be seen. The tongue bone lies within the skull and that too provides attachments from which the forehand-uplifting muscles work.

Riders will find that knowing this gives them an additional incentive to look at the horse's poll – not only to link in telepathically with his thoughts where the spinal cord joins the brain below, but also to watch that the horse's poll remains supple and never 'set' with any unwanted tension or resistance. By correct training methods the lunger and the rider can help the horse to use his poll and his withers as pulleys for the better use of the main muscles of his back and trunk, with the counter-weight of the skull at their front

66

end, and the pulleys of poll and withers to help the strengthening effect of the major muscles of his body.

'Where is the base of the skull?' you may ask, rubbing the top of the nape of your neck and wondering where is the equivalent in the horse. If one remembers that the human is upright (hopefully, in all ways!) while the horse is on all fours (or he should be!), it is easy to understand that whereas in humans the base is located at the bottom of the skull, the equivalent part of the equine skull is at the top. Thus the nape of the horse's neck runs, as does the human nape, from his occipital bone to the axis bone at the top of his spine, i.e. in the poll area.

*The spine*

The strong bones of the spine, the vertebrae, provide a protective tunnel for the spinal cord, the 'trunk road' of the horse's entire nervous system which runs from its headquarters in the brain back to the tail and by 'side roads' to the extremities of the limbs and to all parts of his body. The almost grotesque shape of the horse's spine never ceases to make me marvel that any horse ever manages to go on the bit and in a good form! Figure 2 shows this shape and provides the names of the different portions of the spine. These are of interest as they provide clues for location when considering muscle attachments and uses, but it is better to let the diagram speak for itself rather than filling the page with superfluous text and, worse, Latin names!

The first two vertebrae have special names because they have quite individual shapes, formations and uses. These are the atlas and the axis bones, and during all training they should be considered together with the nuchal crest as the poll area. By means of correct work, the ligaments and muscles in the poll area can be strengthened and suppled, so that they can be employed by the horse as he learns to use the weight of his skull with a leverage and pulley effect to lift the front of his trunk up between his shoulder-blades, to obtain a strong and vibrant connection through his back and thereby find a better balance and way of moving due to a lightened forehand and an improved engagement of his hindlegs.

A fact which should be borne in mind when working a horse on the lunge or under the rider is that very little lateral movement is possible between the thoracic and lumbar vertebrae while the sacral vertebrae are fused into one large, strong bone and have no bending facility at all, although by the horse's muscular form a slight bending seems apparent. If an impossible bend is forced upon a horse by an ignorant trainer using over-tight side reins or some gadget, horses may try to escape the pain by resorting to working in an uncomfortable or unnatural way; this can prove to be over-taxing and thus destructive, mentally and physically. There is no quicker way of destroying the beauty of a horse's natural gaits than allowing a mixture of ignorance, impatience and force into the training of any horse or pony.

*The tail*

The carriage of the last 15–22 vertebrae will reveal much valuable information to the trainer, if he looks for it. In its simplest form, the horse's tail is often used as a rudder, an adjunct to the balancing pole of the head and neck at the front end of the spine. When they are first worked on the lunge and again under the rider, young horses often seem to lose the animation of their tails, which hang down like a damp flag close to the horse's buttocks, and may even flap forward between their hocks.

This situation will soon change with correct schooling, and thus a horse's tail carriage is a reliable gauge of the quality of the training. As the horse gains confidence, strength and a true connection through his back, he will 'wear his tail' (a lovely descriptive expression from Ireland) and, as he carries it clear of his body, it will swing, as a result of a flowing movement through his spine to the tip of his tail, in time with each hind leg as it treads on the ground.

A horse will also use his tail as a form of body language to display well-being, pleasure, worry, aggravation, resistance, pain or apathy.

### The rib cage

There are 18 thoracic vertebrae with 18 ribs springing from them to form a protective cage for the horse's heart and lungs as well as for the bulk of his digestive and circulatory systems.

The lower portions of the ribs are cartilaginous. The first eight of these ribs, are known as true and they are very important because they are firmly joined onto and hold up the breast bone (sternum) which itself forms the substantial floor of the horse's chest.

### The sternum

The sternum resembles the hull of an old wooden war ship. In fact it is made up of a collection of small bones joined into one breast bone. It is literally the base of the weighty parcel of the front of the trunk. Both the sternum and the rib cage provide attachments for many of the muscles which need to be developed in ridden horses in order that they may be stronger and more efficient. These muscles have a most important function to perform, that of supporting and lifting up the front of the horse's trunk when he has to carry a rider-burden and thereby they can enable the horse to find better balance and an easy self-carriage under his rider.

## The appendicular skeleton – the limbs

As well as providing supports for the horse's body, the four limbs provide the horse's means of locomotion.

### The fore limbs (the thoracic limbs)

1. *The shoulder-blade (scapula or blade bone).* These large, flat and long, triangular-shaped bones lie, with an upward and backward slant from the point of the shoulder to the withers, one on either side of the front part of the rib cage.

Although skeletally the horse's shoulder-blades are not attached to the rib cage, muscularly they are attached and in turn, they themselves provide attachments for many very important muscles for hoisting the front of the trunk up between the shoulder-blades, as well as being part of the horse's locomotive system. By nature, the main actions of all these muscles are for respiration and support; however, the trainer can develop them to enable the horse to carry a rider with greater ease and to move with more quality in all his gaits, but this takes knowledge, experience and feel, as well as patience, understanding and time.

2. *The humerus or arm.* The humerus, the equivalent to the human upper arm, lies between the point of the horse's shoulder and his elbow; it forms a part of both joints. The humerus is one of the shortest and strongest bones in the horse's body and it provides numerous attachment points for many major muscles of the forehand and trunk.

If a horse is in good condition the location, if not the existence, of the arm is concealed by well-developed and bulky muscles.

3. *The lower part of the limbs*, i.e. those parts of the limbs which lie below the knees and below the hocks, on all four limbs. It should be remembered that all long bones remain cartilaginous at their extremities until the horse is five, or more.

The human has two collar bones, one on each side at the top of his chest, to provide a firm attachment for the upper limbs to the trunk at the top of the sternum. Riders know more about collar bones than many other members of their species as these are the bones which are most frequently broken in riding accidents! If the lunger will remember that his horse has no collar bones, it will highlight his need for developing the muscles under the shoulder-blades by good and thoughtful work.

Young horses especially are weak, nervous and uncoordinated, which often causes them to swing the lower part of their limbs in an erratic manner. This may result in them injuring their legs with their opposite feet. It is for this reason that horses should wear brushing boots on all four of their lower limbs when they are lunged.

*The hind limbs (the pelvic limbs)*

Unlike the fore limbs, the horse's hind limbs are attached skeletally very securely to his spine, so the propulsive power stemming from his two hind limbs is linked directly into his axial skeleton.

1. *The pelvis.* The landmarks by which you can identify the area containing the pelvic girdle are the following. The top line runs from the point of the croup, immediately behind the loins, to the top of the tail. The width is measured from the outer edges of the two points of the hips (those which you must *never* knock on a doorway). The side lines run from the points of the hips to the rear-most points of the buttocks.

The exact symmetry of all these points should be checked regularly from behind as any misalignment here is indicative of related problems further forward along the horse's spine. It is most unfair to expect a horse to work if his skeleton is 'out of sync.'.

Here's a cautionary note concerning this part of the horse's anatomy. The three large bones which together comprise the pelvic girdle are not joined at birth; they start to fuse when the horse is two years old and as with all his long bones, the cartilaginous joints do not ossify until the horse is four-and-a-half to five-and-a-half years of age, or later in some warm-bloods. It is therefore dangerous to tax a young horse with too much weight on his back and too much work of any sort before he is five years old. He may look mature enough before that age, especially if he has come on well, but obviously it is wisest to wait until the cartilages which will do so have turned into bone.

2. *The thigh bone (femur)*. This is the largest and strongest long bone in the horse's skeletal structure. It provides a great many 'anchorages' for numerous strong and powerful muscles. As with the other stout long bone, the humerus, the strength of the massive muscles for which it provides so many attachments can shatter the bone when the horse is asked to produce a super-equine effort such as he does when racing. If the muscles lose their correct synchronization for even a part of one second; their opposing massive strengths are too much for the bones to withstand.

3. *The shin bones (tibia and fibula)*. These two bones are the equivalent of the human shin, which also consists of two bones: the fibula is the smaller, and is relatively smaller still in the horse. Both bones are important for their length, angulation and support as well as for the muscle attachments they provide.

4. *The hock (tarsus)*. The hock joint consists of six short bones of varying sizes and shapes, arranged in three layers, cushioned by cartilage and bound together by ligaments. The horse's hocks, having so many mini-joints and often being stressed by the work he is asked to perform, are extremely vulnerable to sprains, wear, inflammation and consequent bony deposits which in turn can form the dreaded spavin – the 'spanner in the works' of the hock joint, and often of the horse himself. Lungers beware! Never cause wear and tear by working young horses too hard, too long or on circles which are too small or on a surface which is slippery or uneven.

5. *The feet*. There is an old adage which says 'No foot no horse!' Take great care of them! The feet must be kept in a true shape and balance by an expert farrier, and in good condition by careful husbandry at home.

## MUSCLES

Now that we understand a little of the bones of the matter, we may go forward to a brief study of physiology.

The development of the musculature will always reflect the quality of a horse's training. A number of show horses have disappointing action due to an excess of fat and insufficient muscular development to carry their riders and move under them with a free elegance. Some competition horses look over-lean; whereas it is true that they are not fat, they also lack sufficient volume of muscle. Horses need to be fed well and to be worked like a human athlete with many hours of thoughtful, skilled and caring work. It must never be forgotten that horses thrive best when they are happy.

It becomes very easy to spot a horse whose 'outline' has been forced by artificial means; they have peculiar muscles which stand out above the normally shaped musculature. It is only possible to differentiate between the 'peculiar' and the 'normal' if the latter has been studied. As mentioned in the Introduction, although I am quite happy to use the word 'outline' to describe an incorrect image, I always use 'form'

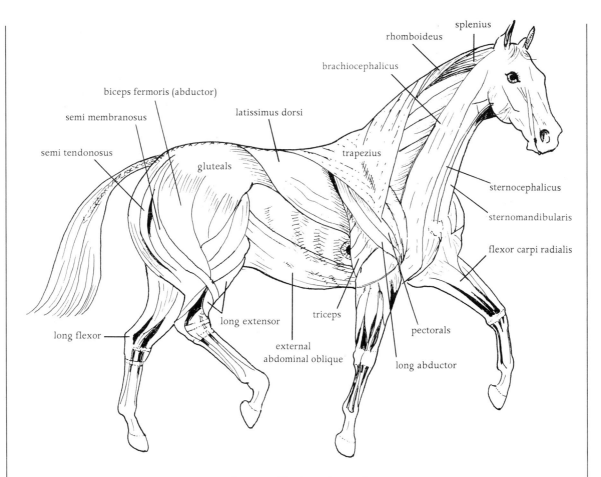

splenius

rhomboideus

brachiocephalicus

biceps fermoris (abductor)

semi membranosus

latissimus dorsi

semi tendonosus

trapezius

gluteals

sternocephalicus

sternomandibularis

flexor carpi radialis

long extensor

triceps

long flexor

pectorals

external
abdominal oblique

long abductor

Figure 4 *The 'muscle map'.*

when describing a horse who looks happy, well, fit and in good condition and who has been trained to carry and move under his rider with balance, poise and a beauty of movement in all three of his basic gaits. To me an 'outline' is just that, a superficial tracing around the outside edges of the horse, whereas the 'form' is viewed with a sculptor's eye combined with that of a gymnast coach and a master of ballet. 'Form' encompasses the whole horse from his skeleton outwards, rather than a mere outer trace-line.

There is no need to feel scared or put off in any way by the formal names of the bones and muscles. In fact, all the names provide accurate clues to the muscles' positions, attachments and functions which can be helpful memory aids. It is useful to know exactly where the muscles are in order that you can see them developing and enhancing the horse's form as they do so. I hope the drawings which accompany this chapter will give you a feel for what to look for when you work your horse on the lunge.

You must know a little of the names and functions of the ligament and muscle-map. Careful and oft-repeated reference to drawings of the superficial and the deeper muscles of the horse is essential for every would-be horse trainer and instructor. Although the horse is sub-divided into regions it is better to consider the map as a whole rather than regionally.

## The skull

The horse's skull contains and protects his brain, the governor of the whole of his nervous system and the receiver of his tele-pathic understanding of his equine and his human friends.

The other vital physiological facts concern-ing the horse's skull, are that it is compara-tively large and heavy and that the base of the horse's skull provides strong attach-ments or anchorages for many of the main trunk muscles or their associated muscles.

As in the human, the horse's head, com-pared with the rest of him, is an extremely heavy part of his body; however, by using and working the bones, joints, ligaments, tendons and muscles of the horse's body, together with the hidden forces of gravity and centrifuge, the head itself can be employed as a counter-weight to improve the efficiency and grace of the horse's posture and movement. Lungers and riders should consider the use of their heads and the connective ligaments and muscles in a similar way, for the good of their posture and general health as well as for the efficien-cy of their work with their horses.

At the base of both the human and the equine skulls there is a particularly vital area called the nuchal crest; the importance of this area of the skull can be appreciated from the list of ligaments and muscles which have their origin there.

## The supraspinous ligament

This is one of the most interesting and influential ligaments. It runs from the nuchal crest at the highest point of the top bone (occipital) of the skull, from whence it follows the top line of the spine to the croup (sacrum). This extremely strong ligament is attached to all of the vertebrae and supports them for its entire length.

The supraspinous ligament is sub-divided into two parts, front and rear. The front portion (ligamentum nuchae) is worthy of extra consideration as it is a most extraor-dinary, powerful, elasticated piece of 'apparatus' and is of the greatest impor-tance to the posture of the horse when he is worked on the lunge or when ridden.

The ligamentum nuchae runs from the base of the skull (at the top of the skull, remember!) to the back of the withers where it becomes the non-elastic portion known as the lumbo-dorsal ligament. The ligamentum nuchae itself consists of two very different parts. The top part, the funicular, resembles a strong and slightly elastic cable which runs from the top of the skull to behind the withers. Where this cable runs over the middle portion of the horse's neck it has an additional develop-ment, called the lamella, which consists of long, frond-like branches which descend rather like octopus legs and are firmly inserted into the vertebrae, which at that part of the neck have a rather off-putting ewe-necked overall shape.

The ligamentum nuchae is most important in the re-arranging of the horse's balance and his way of responding to the rider. It is supplied with underlying protective padding (bursa) at the two pulley areas, at the poll and the withers, the two points which otherwise could suffer wear and cause discomfort when the horse's training is advanced towards greater demands of elevation, collection and bending.

As a matter of interest, this area, the equivalent to the horse's poll, is of extreme importance for human posture, poise, movement, lifting and for health (self-help to prevent curvature of the spine). 'Stretch the nape of your neck' is always a good starter for the day, and a reminder throughout it, especially when you are tired.

The lumbo-dorsal ligament, the rear portion of the supraspinous ligament, runs from the back of the withers to the sacrum at the croup. This portion resembles a strong, non-elastic fibrous cord; it is attached to the tops of the vertebrae and supports, aligns and organizes the spine and the spinal cord within its protective, bony channel.

*The fasciae*

Before considering the actual muscles, we should pause to think about the fasciae, which are present all over the horse's body beneath the outer covering of the skin. Fasciae are like blankets consisting of sheets of fibrous, connective tissues which bind together the bones and muscles with action, reaction and interaction at superficial and deeper layers throughout the horse's body.

Both the superficial and the deep layers of the fasciae of the neck have an important connective action for many of the uplifting muscles of the horse's forehand, as they extend from the nuchal crest and ligamentum nuchae to the tongue (hyoid) bone and the extensor muscles of the spine, and are firmly attached to the first rib and to the front (cariniform) cartilage of the sternum. The collective duties of the fasciae do not stop there, since they also have influences on the major muscles responsible for carriage and movement.

## The major trunk muscles

The main 'continents' in the ligament and muscle-map are the longissimus dorsi, the latissimus dorsi and the splenius muscles, which govern all areas of the horse's trunk, from his neck to his croup, and the neck muscles themselves (all twenty-four pairs of them!), the trapezius muscle of the neck, the withers, shoulders and the back, the external abdominal oblique muscles of the belly, the diaphragm internally and the gluteal muscles of the hindquarters.

There are two groups of muscles which are very undeveloped in all young horses, and about which many riders and trainers are uninformed. However, as correct gymnastic training can increase these muscles to nearly twice their initial size and strength, knowledge of their usefulness in the ridden horse is of the utmost importance. Of course, I am talking about the adductor and abductor muscles. The names are very easy to learn if it is remembered that to 'add' something brings it towards you and to 'abduct' takes it away. From this, it is readily understood that adductor muscles pull the limbs towards the trunk and abductor muscles pull them away.

*Pammy asks Calendo to leg yield to the right at walk.*

This in turn makes it easier to understand the value of work on large circles and of the two most basic and easy of all of the school movements, those of turns on the forehand and of leg yielding. These are both wonderful exercises for developing the abductor and adductor muscles in the very early stages of a young horse's training and also for suppling up those same muscles when warming up an older horse, before he goes on to work at more advanced lateral movements which require collection and bending. These two exercises are also excellent for removing excess tension from within the horse's body.

With the combined knowledge of the location and the actions of at least the main bones, joints and muscles, the educated lunger and rider can help the young horse to increase the stability of his equilibrium through development of the required muscles. By skilful work on the lunge and later when ridden, provided that the young horse has no glaring conformation faults, a good trainer can transform that horse into a notable riding horse for pleasure riding or for any of the competitive fields. In the latter case, which field will depend on each individual horse's liking as well as his natural talent.

# 7

# *Training a Young Horse to Lunge*

The manner in which the young horse is introduced to the lunge is vitally important; the more carefully and thoroughly the preparations are carried out, the better will be the whole of the horse's training and his career. He should be accustomed to and confident in the following: to being handled and to a combined stable and grazing routine, to being groomed and trimmed and to being led about to either hand equally, to seeing strange sights and sounds, to having his feet picked out and trimmed, to wearing a tail bandage, to seeing traffic and being led over poles and over uneven ground, to learning to concentrate on his trainer's wishes in the lesson and while other horses are tended or worked in close proximity, and later to being led from another 'schoolmaster' horse.

When he is two and a half years old, the young horse should be taught to wear a lungeing roller. The introduction of a roller cannot be done too carefully as many young horses will get into an immediate and real panic if they feel their body is entrapped within a solid contraption such as a stout, tight leather roller. Although native ponies and unhandled wild young horses are the most susceptible to panic in this situation, the introduction of a roller or a saddle to any young horse is full of potential danger to humans and equines alike. Trainer, owner and assistant must appreciate that this stage of training a young horse can be fraught with danger. It is essential that the good preparatory work described above has been done and accepted by the young horse, and that the introduction of the roller is presented as a perfectly normal occurrence but with every precaution taken. For example, it is best to select a sensible location for the first introduction – a foaling box, a small barn or an indoor school are all reasonably safe. A small loose box is not safe, as there is far too big a risk that if the young horse panics he will trap and hurt someone and if he goes berserk he may injure himself, even fatally, on one of the walls. The trainer should always have a good and well-trained assistant who is equally known and trusted by the horse as is the trainer himself.

As a preliminary exercise the handler should make use of the horse's back when he rolls up the tail bandage. After a day or two he can encircle the front of the horse's trunk, around the front of the saddle and the girth area, with the bandage, the ends held in his hands, and give it gentle tugs before he rolls up the bandage. The handler should reward the youngster immediately for putting up with the new and seemingly dangerous encroachment on his body's freedom. Any sign of worry or excess tension on the horse's part should be a clear indication to the trainer that danger lurks, that he must 'gang warily' and should proceed with extreme care – any impatience after such a warning could have disastrous results.

The training roller should be well padded with a comfortably fitted breast girth to prevent it from sliding back too far. Great care must be taken at all times that the roller is only tightened very gently each time the lungeing roller and later, the saddle, is put on. Sudden and too-tight girthing can cause fear and pain and a severe reaction in many young horses – memories which some of them never forget. Such a negligent trainer-fault may cause total panic and a fatal injury.

## Timing

As in all work with horses, the training stages of lungeing are based on understanding the horse's point of view, combined with a logical mental and physical development and progression. Although the preliminaries may be introduced when the young horse is two and a half, he should not be given serious training or work on the lunge until he is at least three and a half or four years old. Generally speaking, the bigger the horse and the less Thoroughbred blood in his veins, the later his lunge-training should begin, as larger, warm-blooded horses take longer to mature and therefore the risk of an injury to their long bones and joints is greater.

With regard to the time-span of any of

these stages, it is impossible to lay down any hard-and-fast rules as each individual horse has his own acceptance rate. Progress through the programmes should be finely gauged, to retain his interest on the one hand and on the other hand not to overface him, mentally or physically.

The actual lungeing part of a lunge lesson for a young horse should not exceed 20 minutes but the whole lesson should be extended gradually to one hour of education. The extra time should be devoted to training of some sort such as picking up feet, walking in hand around strange places and objects, being led over undulating ground and so on. All of these and other similar exercises will establish and reinforce his worldliness and confidence. Always remember to finish on a high note and always reward promptly and generously.

### Stage one

Leading in hand. One of the chief aims of the trainer in stage one is to build up the horse's trust in him and his confidence in general. This is a most important stage in the young horse's training, his first introduction to work. In order to build a strong rapport with the young horse, the trainer must use a carefully judged mixture of kind understanding and firmness based on a system of reward and correction. He should talk to the horse as a friend in an adult manner. Horses learn to interpret their trainer's personality through the tone of voice – nursery language does not create safe respect.

The trainer should lead the young horse in a well-fitted cavesson, with a long leading

*The trainer should concentrate on maintaining a good rapport with the horse. Talland Cavalier is well aware that there is an assistant walking behind.*

rein attached to the centre ring on the front of the noseband. An assistant should follow behind, keeping his distance tactfully whilst ready to coax the young horse along with a quiet movement of a long stick should this be necessary. The whip or stick should be carried discreetly hidden against the outline of the assistant's body; it should be long to extend the assistant's reach, not to increase the intensity of the hit. This leading in hand should be done equally on both sides of the horse and the trainer should talk sensibly to him, using this stage to introduce the first words of command, i.e. 'Walk on' and 'Whoa!', 'Steady' and 'Stand still'. The assistant should be like a model child, only speaking when spoken to, and then quietly and unobtrusively. He should support and never interrupt the mental bond being built up between the young horse and his trainer.

The horse should be encouraged to walk alongside his trainer, shoulder to shoulder. The trainer should concentrate on maintaining a good rapport with the horse so that he teaches him the two-way link-up of the thought aid which forms the foundation for human–equine partnerships and so that a strong mutual understanding is formed between the two beings. The leading-rein should be long enough to enable the trainer to hold on to the horse should he be startled, and so that he never learns how to escape.

The trainer should hold the rein approximately 16–60 cm (6 in–2 ft) from the horse's head. The hand which is nearest to the horse should be carried with its back uppermost, the rein being held out of the heel of the hand with a firm but light hold.

The trainer should use the tip of his thumb on the rein, as when riding, to prevent the rein from sliding out through his hand, and if the horse tries to pull away or to play up, he should turn his wrist with the little finger part of his hand moved towards his body whilst keeping his elbow close to his side. This is the most secure grasp in a tricky situation.

The trainer should carry the remainder of the leading-rein, neatly coiled, together with his whip, in the hand which is furthest away from the horse. Initially the whip should be a schooling or stiff dressage whip of medium length; later he can substitute the schooling whip for his lunge-whip with the thong furled and secured.

The trainer should also carry and give some form of reward, so that the horse really enjoys his work and gains confidence as quickly as possible. It is important that horses are rewarded throughout their training as this is one of the quickest ways to accelerate the learning process. (Have some chopped carrots and apples ready in your pocket in a small plastic bag.)

This leading-in-hand stage of the young

horse's education should be continued at regular intervals during the first 1–3 years of his training. During the latter part, he should be led from a well-trained horse so that he can become accustomed to seeing a human being on a higher plane, level with his back. He should also learn how to improve the dexterity of his footwork by being led over undulating ground with dips, rises and small ditches.

*Stage two*

Personally, I do not think there is any advantage to be gained by putting a bit in the young horse's mouth until he understands and is obedient when being led about to either hand and when being lunged. If a young horse plays up when he is bitted too early, there is a great risk of him bruising or permanently damaging his mouth – and his memory. The pain from a bit will not stop a horse, often it will only serve to make him more frightened. However, do make sure that you have sufficient weight, muscle power, agility and expertise to hold the young horse you are training. If you lack any of these qualities then it is better to send the young horse to an expert to start him for you, so that his training and his life will be built on sure foundations.

Lungeing on a circle may now commence, usually on the left rein to start with as most horses find this easier. The trainer and an assistant must work very closely as a team. The trainer has the lunge-rein in his left hand and the whip in his right hand. After they have walked the horse forward together, the trainer takes up a stand in the centre of the circle while the

*The trainer and his assistant work closely as a team. At first the assistant walks round on the horse's inner side, acting as a protector and translator.*

assistant stays close to the horse's head on the horse's left, inner side, with his right hand holding a short rein looped through the back of the cavesson and his left hand holding a short whip in case he might need it for emphasis or correction, as he leads the horse on a circle around the trainer. From this position the assistant can act as the silent translator of the trainer's wishes and commands to the horse and, in the case of a nervous horse, he also forms a kind of barrier which protects the young horse from the fierce person with the whip!

The majority of work at this stage should be done at walk. The assistant should also carry some form of reward which he should mete out as the trainer says 'Good boy' at every halt. The trainer's voice should be the only one heard by the horse. The assistant must not interrupt this communication with chatter of his own.

## Stage three

When the horse goes around the trainer on a circle to either hand confidently and steadily and halts to the command 'Whoa!', the trainer can move on to the next stage where the assistant walks on the outer side of the horse, from where he provides a supportive but less dominant influence for the

*The assistant walks on the outside. The horse seems to say, 'I believe that man in the middle is taking over, but I'm so glad you are still assisting him – and me.'*

young horse. The trainer now has an uninterrupted, and therefore stronger, direct influence on the horse.

As before, at this transitional stage, the assistant holds a rein looped through the back of the cavesson while the horse becomes accustomed to the fact that there is no longer any protection between himself and the trainer. As before, the assistant assists the horse to understand and obey the trainer's commands under these new conditions.

When the first part of stage three is established, and the horse is confident and obedient, the trainer will tell the assistant

that next time they walk forward he wishes him to release the rein from the cavesson and to walk forward, calmly and boldly, at a tangent away from the horse. It is important that the assistant surreptitiously increases the tempo of his walking as he lets go, as this is a moment when a horse can feel nervous at the departure of his friend, combined with a feeling of freedom, and he may move forward more quickly himself. If the young horse's movement is quicker than that of the assistant he may be tempted to lash out as he passes close to him and he could kick him severely with both hind heels. I have never known this to happen, but my

*The young horse is really concentrating on his trainer; in fact his left ear seems to have grown longer! The assistant gives the young horse a reassuring glance as she strides away at a tangent.*

assistants have been well trained. To be forewarned is to be forearmed.

The trainer can now start to work the young horse directly and on his own. It is useful to have the assistant present with the reward-bag to ensure that the horse stays out on the circle track when he halts and does not turn in to go and get his reward from the trainer in the centre of the circle. If the assistant gives the reward, it makes it easier for the horse to understand that he should come to a square halt and wait for the reward to come to him. The horse should learn to stay out on a circle, the track of which should be as

nearly perfect as possible. The assistant should make several unobtrusive changes to his position after the horse has moved forward so that the latter learns to obey his trainer whenever he commands 'Whoa!' rather than walking on to a set halting-place.

A trainer who is very experienced and who has a way with horses will often prefer to start young horses in the lungeing phase of their career without an assistant. A strong rapport and a fine sense of timing is of the essence in all work with horses, especially with young horses. These two qualities need to be particularly spot-on when

*The young horse is working for and by himself, and responding confidently to his trainer's instructions.*

teaching young horses to lunge. An experienced lunger will often find that, due to one or more possible causes, his assistant is too slow off the mark at a vital moment, and is more of an impediment than a help to the lesson, which becomes far more difficult for the horse to understand. Trainer and horse must work in close unison; if the horse has the full input of the trainer's thoughts, words and actions, this leads to clear understanding and ready learning of the lessons being given to him.

If the trainer is sufficiently experienced to start young horses with their lunge lessons single-handedly, he should have carried out most of the lessons on leading in hand, shoulder to shoulder, to either hand himself, so that he knows absolutely that this part of the training has been correct. He will also then be certain that the young horse respects, trusts and understands him, and that he has learned to obey the commands and actions required of him for 'Walk-on', 'Steady', 'Whoa', 'Stand still', 'Move-over' and 'Trot-on'.

Before lungeing on a circle, the trainer should teach the horse to walk–halt–walk when led from a distance of 1–3 m (3–10 ft) from the horse's shoulders. This can be taught alongside a guiding fence, along a drive or in an indoor school. The latter is best for concentration and it is safer for that reason; if a pheasant gets up or some unexpected happening frightens a young horse when the trainer is 2–3 m (6–10 ft) away from him, in his fright or panic the young horse could easily swing round on the lengthened rein and deliver a dangerous kick at the trainer in order to escape from his restraint and the supposed danger. There is no worse place to be than at the very end of the horse's hindleg when he really kicks out, as then one is hit with the full force of the horse's power, which invariably leads to shattered bones or worse.

When lungeing, the trainer should keep his two feet on the spot as nearly as possible in order that he may work the horse on a true circle track around him. With the lunge-rein attached to the centre ring on the front of the cavesson, fitted as a drop noseband, the trainer can use his rein aids to work on the lowest, comfortable part of the horse's skull and by skilful play on this very heavy bony mass, he can use its lever effect to help the horse to supple the joints between the skull, the atlas and axis, at the poll. This has a softening effect throughout the whole of the horse's musculature with an immediate improvement to his form and movement.

The size of the circle and the length of the lunge-rein will all depend on the horse's acceptance of the work, his natural ability and the exercises being used. As a lunge-rein is about 10 m (33 ft) in length, there will nearly always be some extra length to be kept in reserve. This should be folded carefully and neatly into the lunger's rein hand, as described in detail in Chapter 4 (page 33).

Some young horses are impetuous and enjoy feeling that just perhaps the trainer cannot now enforce obedience, that they are out of reach. They seem almost to test the trainer when he says 'Steady' and 'Whoa!' by appearing suddenly to be totally deaf as they continue round the trainer at a brisk trot! However, the experienced trainer will understand and will remain calm as he waits and then tries out alternative strategies to change subtly the horse's way of thinking so that he wants to obey and thus to please. Under no circumstances must the trainer get ruffled and certainly he must not get cross.

The first alternative method to halt a reluctant horse is to allow him more rein and space in which to practise lengthened strides, after which an unfit horse will soon wish to slow down, so the transition is made very willingly. The second method is to bring the horse a little closer to the trainer by decreasing the size of the circle, which intensifies the work in a different manner; it also makes the trainer's mind, body movement and the rein controls more effective. Sometimes with this method the trainer may find that if he exchanges the rein and the whip for a few moments, so that the whip is in the left hand when lungeing to the left, he can then quietly raise the whip just sufficiently in front of the horse to gain his attention, which is usually enough to underline the trainer's wishes for a slower gait.

An over-impetuous horse, or one who has been badly started and possibly even frightened, may need the third method which is that, by a combination of clever timing, rein- and footwork, the trainer can manoeuvre the horse to come face-to-face with the wall or enclosing fence. When using this last method, which is the most drastic of the three, it is very important that the trainer stands absolutely still when the horse has halted and is thinking about it all as he looks into the wall. This is where the assistant can be such a help, quietly approaching the horse as the trainer keeps telling the horse to stand still and what a good boy he is, while the assistant gives the horse his reward.

Horses usually learn this part of stage three quite quickly and as a trainer it can be very impressive later, if the horses obey a raised whip as a signal to come to a square halt, even from a canter!

The proportion of time that the trainer should spend working the horse in the various gaits will depend on the purpose of the work but, broadly speaking, most of the initial work of a young horse should be done at walk, without side reins and with instant and generous rewards, while he learns to halt and to move forward confidently at a purposeful walk. The young horse gains confidence in his trainer and in the whole activity of lungeing as he learns to obey while practising these easy transitions together with still halts.

A well-fitting snaffle bridle, without reins, may be introduced as the horse settles to the work; it is often helpful to introduce it in the stable first and to allow him to eat a short feed with the bit in his mouth. This accustoms the horse to the presence and feel of the bit in his mouth, and encourages him to move and keep his tongue underneath the bit.

As soon as he is fit enough, the bulk of the horse's work will be carried out at trot; the trainer may well use occasional short periods of canter, the main objective of which will be to improve the quality of the ensuing trot. It is not wise to do too much canter work on the lunge until later when the horse is mature and fitter, as such work tends to put too much strain on the horse's joints. If a young horse is worked to a pitch when all his muscles start to ache then he will be forced to try to find ways to evade working his body and limbs correctly; he will cease to enjoy his work and its quality will deteriorate.

It is always better to arrange the programme so that the trainer gives young horses two short lessons, even as short as 15 minutes lungeing, rather than one longer lesson each day, as not only is this routine less taxing, but also it gives the horse two after-lesson periods for reflection and assimilation of the work.

Although it is possible to start a young horse single-handedly, it is far safer, as well as being easier for the trainer and the horse, if an experienced assistant is present – this could be you. The safety of the assistant is the trainer's responsibility, and when he is training a raw young horse it is essential that he enlists the aid of a competent, lightweight rider to act as his assistant actually to back the young horse. If possible, that rider should have been trained originally by the trainer, as then he will know how to adapt his balance as well as all the finer points of the trainer's methods; he will be quick to establish a good rapport and will use the same commands as well as the same intonations, all of which makes for quicker and easier understanding for the horse. He will also have learned the full and correct use of the six natural aids.

## Stage four

When the horse has learned to keep his balance, rhythm and momentum on a circle, an experienced lunger can then work the horse to improve his form and the quality of the strides at trot and canter, using the trot more than the canter, and the transitions between the two to develop a better quality in the ensuing trot.

To do this the lunger should use the centre line of the school, or if the lungeing area has sufficient width he can work on the diameter line. In this exercise the lunger works on a true circle, for instance at the C end of the centre line, at canter and trot. When the horse settles back into an active trot and is going consistently, the trainer can decide to go for some lengthened strides. By his thinking and his stance he warns the horse that he is going to need something extra from him as the horse goes over the side point before C.

After the horse has moved over the centre line at C, the trainer starts to move straight down the centre line, leading and 'pushing' the horse on a straight line parallel with it. The length of this straight track will depend on the horse's reaction and the trainer's fitness and speed.

As the horse either starts to slow down or deviates inward from the straight line, the trainer asks him to circle, probably near X. He does several circles to re-establish the quality and consistency of the gait and then repeats the lengthening part of the exercise towards the A marker, where again he makes several circles before bringing the horse to a halt and rewarding him. The trainer should change the rein and repeat

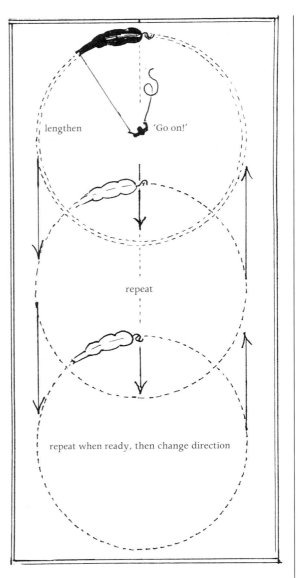

Figure 5 *Working the horse down the school to stimulate interest and to lengthen the stride.*

the exercise, working back down the centre line to the C end of the school.

The trainer should use his discretion over the use of side reins. They are useful to assist the trainer's control of a large, 'bolshie' or spoiled horse, or to improve the work of a more experienced horse, but should not be necessary at this stage of a young horse's training.

As long as the trainer is sufficiently skilled, he should not need to resort to side reins which may impede the suppling and balancing work with the horse's skull, described above. The advantages and disadvantages of side reins are discussed in detail on pages 25–32, but it is such an important issue that some salient points bear repeating here.

• Side reins should be fitted loosely at first, so that the young horse has to stretch forward to seek a contact with the bit, and can learn to respect them and 'give' in his jaw, poll and neck to their constraint.

• Side reins should never be adjusted tightly in an endeavour to force a horse into a set 'shape'; they should allow him room to develop his musculature as well as his understanding and his movement.

• Too short side reins may make a horse back off rather than seek a contact with the bit. Enforcing too much contact, too soon, will often cause a young horse to rear, lose his balance and fall over backwards, due to the sudden pain in his mouth. He will remember this abuse all his life, and may develop into a rearer and become dangerous to ride.

• Side reins should never be fitted to 'pull the pony's or horse's nose in'. They are only of benefit to a horse's training when he is being worked correctly on a lunge-rein, being encouraged to move forward, towards the bit. The practice of fitting tight side reins on to any horse when he is standing still in his loose box has nothing to recommend it – in fact it has detrimental effects, causing muscle ache, cramp and mental and physical pain.

Work over ground-poles should be introduced into stage four of the young horse's training on the lunge (see Chapter 9). Side reins, if used, should always be removed for this work.

# 8

# Backing the Young Horse

When the trainer feels that the young horse is going confidently on the lunge, has learned to trust and respect his trainer and to obey his commands, and that his physique has developed sufficiently to support the weight of a light-weight rider on his back, he should make all the arrangements that are necessary to back the young horse.

At the end of a lungeing session which has been reasonably taxing, the trainer should replace the roller with a saddle. It is best to use a saddle which is well worn-in, with a sound tree, which fits the horse well and is comfortable for the rider. It should be equipped with an old-fashioned type of hunting breastplate, which is essential to ensure that neither the saddle nor the girth slide back, and it also provides the rider with three possible hand-grips should he require them. A breastplate is far better for this latter use than is a neckstrap, which is most unstable and can be guaranteed to slip round if a horse bucks and drops one of his shoulders.

A young horse who is very croup-high and who lacks the muscle necessary to keep the saddle back behind his shoulder-blades will need a crupper until he develops the correct form of musculature. The horse will have been accustomed to wearing a crupper with his roller, but he should be lunged in the saddle and crupper for several days to acclimatize him to the new feeling before putting up the rider.

Backing should be a gradual, logical progression of the young horse's training programme, carried out in peace and quiet so that he has full opportunity to accept the strange new sensations with confidence. Any form of excitement or alarm must be avoided: a rodeo performance may be thrilling for spectators but it is disastrous for the young horse's training.

Providing that the young horse has been well handled, cared for and nurtured and his training has been started correctly, the trainer will hold the young horse on a shortened lunge-rein while an additional assistant gives the rider-assistant a good and careful leg up so that he lies across the saddle. This should be done from each side equally at the end of each lunge session after one to three weeks of training on the lunge. The rider-assistant should pat the horse on his far shoulder and rib-cage while giving meaningful praise. He should not sit up yet as by so doing he may give the young horse a fright, set back his training for several weeks – and hospitalize the rider. There should be no cause for the horse to try to buck when he is first backed. However, if there is the slightest doubt in your mind concerning a young

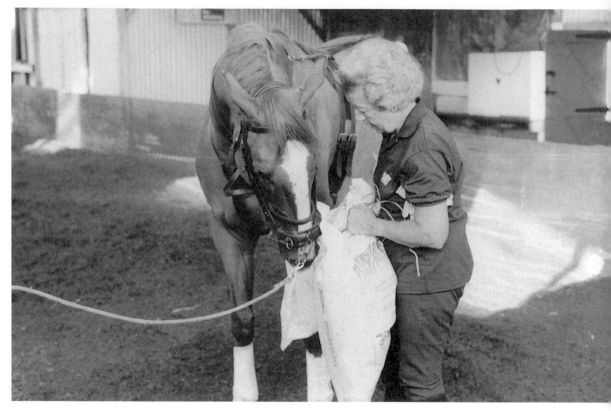

*Talland Cavalier meets 'George' for the first time – 'Curiouser and curiouser'!*

horse's temperament, particularly if he has previously been badly started, if he displays a lack of confidence or if he shows even a small degree of being either nervous or resentful, it is as well to include an introductory phase to the backing by the use of what we refer to at Talland as 'George'.

'George' consists of two sacks filled with straw! The sacks are tied securely at their tops, to each other and to the D's of the saddle, with some cord, which can then be attached to the roller or surcingle that is fitted over the saddle and its protective cover. The two lower ends of each of the sacks are then attached to and under the girth at stirrup level. Do make sure that

'George' awaits the horse in the indoor school or alternative enclosed area being used for lungeing. It would be a grave mistake to put 'George' on in the loose-box.

The great advantage of using 'George' prior to backing the young horse is that, providing your knowledge of knots is good enough, he *cannot* be bucked off. Horses can emulate a champion bucking bronco if they wish but they soon learn that there is no point at all in trying to buck off the substitute rider-burden who is so firmly attached to the saddle. The young horse's disobedience cannot succeed, and what is more he learns this valuable lesson without any risk to human limb or life.

*He accepts the strange burden without question.*

Possibly the most important part for 'George' to play, apart from being used with horses who have already been frightened by being started badly, is in the case of children's ponies which are too small for adults to ride. Ponies being nearer to nature than their more civilized, larger equine relations, are particularly good at bucking and really like to score successes in the number of times they can empty their saddles. This is disastrous for their training and does not do the nerves of their young riders any good at all – to say nothing of their parents' nerves! When a young pony has got used to 'George' in his simplest version, it is advisable to develop him into a special 'pony's' version; this has the addition of noise, i.e. stones in tins and bushy twigs with bits of fertilizer bag, the first giving rattles and the second giving rustles, which are excellent preambles to the sort of noises that are made by the contents of children's pockets.

## Methods for mounting

There are two methods for mounting the young horse, either using a mounting block or an assistant who gives the rider a leg up. It is good for the young horse if he is trained to accept both methods.

*a  Body language says it all. Horse: 'What on earth are those doing there?' Assistant: 'Come on – it's quite all right.' Trainers: 'What a fuss you are making about nothing.' Note reward at the ready.*

*b  The mounting block is accepted. Let mounting commence ...*

*c  The young horse looks wary and he moves his left forelimb forward to maintain his balance as the rider starts to put weight on the saddle.*

*d  The young horse finds the mounting block even more scarey from the other side.*

*e  His trainer gives him a reward.*

*f  The horse's expression denotes acceptance of the situation and trust, for which he is again rewarded.*

a

b

d

e

c

f

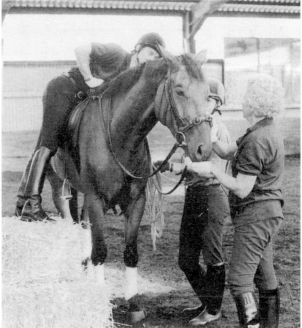

a

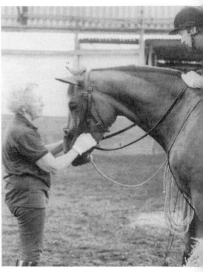

b

*The rider remains keyed-in to his horse's brain as he starts to put weight onto the stirrup.*

*The rider must stay crouching dow*

d

e

*The rider and the person giving the leg up must agree the timing before they start.*

*The rider must be*

c

ver the horse's withers at first.

*Then he can sit upright and the horse is rewarded with praise, a pat and a small titbit.*

f

lsted high enough.

*The rider's foot is put into the stirrup irons.*

For the mounting-block method the horse must be accustomed to standing stock-still next to the mounting block while the rider climbs up and down many times from both sides, rewarding the horse for standing still. A bale of straw makes a useful, safe and natural-looking temporary mounting block placed near a corner in the indoor or outdoor school.

For the leg-up method of mounting, another experienced assistant is required. The first part of the leg up should be practised several times before the rider is actually put up on to the saddle.

It is very important that the rider stays crouched down over the withers and talks to the horse while patting him when he is first put up astride on to his back. The young horse will realize that his rider has done something different with his right leg and he must be given time to accept this change. A rider who sits bolt upright immediately after mounting is bound to give the young horse a nasty shock, and it may not be more than a fraction of a second before the rider gets one too!

On the second day the mounting can be done two or three times with a lungeing interlude in between and plenty of reward; probably on the last occasion, if the horse seems very calm, it will be possible to walk him forward under the rider's weight for a few steps. It must be remembered that the young horse will not yet have developed any muscles for this new task he is being asked to perform, and he will feel very vulnerable as the weight of the rider will upset both his balance and his coordination. Most young horses feel very 'drunk' for these early steps under the rider's weight. The rider must be very experienced, be positive and confident and have a soft and supple seat. A novice rider should *never* attempt to back a young horse, even when assisted. His lack of rapport, balance, ease and suppleness can be very frightening for a sensitive young horse, and the novice rider will not have developed the required high standards of experience and feel or the speedy reactions to enable him to handle any of the highly dangerous situations which may arise, especially if the horse panics. Nothing will make a young horse try to get rid of a rider-burden quicker than a rider whose weight is out of balance, or whose back and hips are stiff. As always, but now even more so, this is a very crucial time for the correct use of the thought and weight aids (see Chapter 2).

The trainer should ensure that everything is done to make the process of backing as safe as possible and a thoroughly natural and easy occurrence from the horse's point of view. Calm, kind and firm is the way.

### Use of the lunge-rein when backing

The young horse's balance and his coordination will have been totally upset by the addition of the weighty burden on his back; not meaning to be rude, but any weight on a horse's back has to be considered unnatural. For this reason in the early backing lessons the young horse should be asked to walk forward only for about five to fifteen steps before he is halted and made a fuss of, and allowed to regain his balance before the short walk is repeated.

His ridden work should be built up gradually until the trainer feels that the task is accepted psychologically and physically by the young horse, and until he is ready to walk forward with the trainer allowing him a little more space on the lunge-rein. It is so important that this phase is not rushed. The pace should be measured by confidence rather than by the calendar. Remember it is the horse's training that needs to show progress rather than the trainer's reputation being enhanced by a speedy result!

If the young horse's owner is sufficiently skilled to be accepted as the rider-assistant, the trainer must confirm that the rider is well-acquainted with the six natural aids of thought, weight, legs, reins, voice and feel, and that he understands how to teach them to the horse and to school him with them thereafter. Gradually the trainer will reduce the volume and content of his instructions, as he allows the rider to increase his influence on the young horse.

The trainer will give the commands and remain in charge at first while the rider sits on the young horse, quietly, supple and in perfect balance. The two people must work in close cooperation with each other with a mutual goal of explaining the new set of signals, the six natural aids, which together they will teach to the horse so that he can understand them and comply with his rider's wishes.

*The young horse is asked to walk forward under his rider-burden. The three-way rapport is most noticeable.*

*The young horse has accepted the situation happily. His rider looks in the mirror to check that the horse looks as good as he feels.*

When the trainer feels the horse has sufficient balance and confidence to carry his rider-burden while moving out on a full-sized lunge circle around him, he should start to hand over his roles of rapport, control and training to the rider. The trainer now becomes an essential translator of the rider's natural aids as the horse works around him on the lunge, mainly at walk at first, then short spells at trot with very carefully correct and tactfully ridden transitions between the two gaits.

At first the rider's main aids will be those of thought, weight (for balance), voice and feel. Initially the rider's voice will be the major link between the rider's control and the horse's understanding of that control; it is imperative at this stage that the rider has good hands and that he hardly uses his rein aids at all, not even for stopping or for turning. The rider may use a light opening rein for guidance but he should never try to steer a young horse with a backward pull – such an action makes absolutely no sense to a young, green or untrained horse.

At this stage the rider should apply his leg aids with much tact and very little action, or he may receive a large re-action! He must be certain that he sits sufficiently to the left when circling to the left and vice versa.

The target of 100 per cent perfect balance cannot be achieved unless the rider shifts his weight and adjusts his seat correctly before and for each change of direction.

As soon as the young horse has learned and understands how to walk forward from halt, to change direction to the right and to the left and will halt willingly and stand quite still when asked to do so, the trainer should suggest that the rider urges the horse forward into a slow trot for a few strides before returning to the gait of walk and a rewarding word of praise and a pat. The rider should remain sitting with soft snd supple hips throughout this exercise.

The gait of trot should be introduced with the rider sitting very softly and to the inside as the horse is worked on an 18 m (59 ft) circle and through smooth and easy transitions. The trainer must watch that the rider never pulls on the reins for down-ward transitions; he should remind him to 'Think, walk and "grow tall" from your waist upwards!' This work should be developed over the next few days until the horse can trot steadily for two or three large circles and will carry out turns and transitions as his rider requests. When the trainer considers the horse is steady enough he may remove the lunge-rein and work the horse and rider around him without it. The trainer's thought aid can be of real assistance to the rider and the horse at this stage. If he rides well enough, the rider may encourage the horse to develop his trot work by skilled use of rising trot.

Reward should be generous and transitions and halts smooth, soft and steady, with emphasis on the stillness of all halts. This is a most important discipline for every horse to be taught from his earliest lessons and woe betide any pupil who 'un-teaches' it!

*The gait of trot should be introduced with the rider sitting very softly and to the inside.*

*When the horse is obedient and confident, the lunge-rein may be removed and he may be given the same work on a large circle.*

The young horse is now ready to be ridden away with further intelligently planned steady work, continuing his education as a well-trained riding horse.

Perhaps I should mention at this stage that not all young horses remain calm and behave like four-legged angels during the first stages of backing. Often the horses who will have the best character to cope with competition stresses will be found to be amongst the naughtiest in the early stages of their training. Horses with a bit of character often resent authority the most, as with many human beings. I have to say that many of our most 'bolshie' students have turned out to have all the qualities required for a team member at international level, and that has proved to be the case with young horses too!

I am convinced, after more years with horses than I care to add up, that horses are not born bad, they are made so by people; by bad training or lack of understanding on the part of the people who have the horses' destiny in their hands but do not appreciate or fulfil their responsibilities.

By careful observation it is usually easy to discover why a horse reacts in an unexpected way. It is always better to go back a stage to confirm the work and regain the horse's confidence rather than being impatient, causing a confrontation and probably a battle to boot.

One of the most easily noticeable signs to look and listen for when halting after a difference of opinion or a more demanding exercise, is that the horse will take in a deeper breath than usual. It is almost as though he does this to gather all the excess tension from within and expel it with the ensuing sigh. Quite often a horse who has become tense will not even accept his favourite titbit until he has given this exhalation.

If a young horse plays up it is senseless to shout at him or hit him – he will only be confused and frightened because he cannot understand such treatment when he is feeling well, freer than when stuck in the confines of his loose box and full of *joie de vivre*. The trainer should enlist the assistance of another expert to help him to lead the boisterous youngster to a safe lungeing area, and lunge the tickle out of his feet; or let him loose in a well-fenced paddock for an hour or two before he is given his lesson. It is so important to understand the young horse's thoughts and feelings at all times, and to look for reasons for so-called 'misbehaviour'.

Of course there are some occasions when the young horse may play up in a wayward or cussed way. A good trainer will always be able to differentiate between misbehaviour which is due to fear or misunderstanding, and that due to wilful disobedience. If the trainer is absolutely certain that the cause of the upset is the latter, then he must déliver a suitable degree of reprimand – always provided that he is in a safe place to do so and that he has arranged everything to his advantage beforehand.

Horses do not suffer from the human failing of false pride. If, therefore, the trainer has the slightest doubt in his mind that he might not succeed with an outright win of any battle which might result from a confrontation, then the wisest and best course for him to follow is to back down, change to a much easier lesson, and wait until the young horse has recovered his confidence, understanding and obedience before attempting a repeat of the work which caused the problem. There is one exception to this training rule, and that is 'nappiness'.

Nappiness is most easily defined as disobedience. From his earliest days the young horse must be taught to obey the rules of his society, whether that is mainly equine or human. This is a natural concept. To be strict about the social rules is not cruel or even slightly unkind as long as all corrections are:

- fair
- immediate
- well-planned
- of exactly the correct proportions to enable the horse to understand that his action was wrong and that a repetition would not be appreciated.

Just as a foal is reprimanded for lack of manners by his mother or other senior member of the herd, so the owner and the trainer must educate the young horse so that he is an acceptable and safe member of his domesticated equine society.

Too often owners who profess to be horse lovers will spoil the foal or young horse who is their pride and joy with too much fuss and too many titbits; these owners will add to the growing problem as they avoid correcting their youngster when he naps, barges, kicks or knocks them over. Such lapses of good manners are mistakes of behaviour and can quickly develop into very dangerous habits, as a result of which the owner could suffer severe injuries. Such leniency or spoiling is no better for a horse than it is for a child. When the spoilt young horse is sent away to school to be trained for his future role in life, he will have a series of rude awakenings ahead if he arrives in the trainer's yard a strong, large and unruly young horse. Whereas if he is already aware that it is both pleasant and worthwhile to respect and to please the human being in charge, he will find his training truly enjoyable.

If, due to a gene from one of his parents or more usually from having been spoiled in his early days, a young horse is nappy on the lunge, he will one day – not necessarily at the beginning of his lunge training – decide he does not see why he should go round to the right (or to the left). It is very important that this trait is spotted and corrected immediately. Quite often an intelligent horse will try a nap when he is getting bored while he is being lunged by an assistant who is just a little too slow to anticipate his mischievous action. Inevitably a battle of wits will ensue and the horse, being the stronger, will be the victor! It is important to warn assistants that they must report all signs of nappiness or disobedience at once as it will take more than one person to make a sure correction of this major trait in his early training.

There are three main routes of evasion open to the horse; he may nap by turning into face the lunger and immediately return to the left rein, often with a defiant scurry at his success. He may pull backwards, or he may nap by making a very quick turn outwards, thereby getting the rein over his neck. All of these are occasions when side reins will help to keep the horse straight. It is essential that the trainer retains a calm and positive attitude; on no account must he lose his temper in the slightest degree.

If the the horse turns either inwards or outwards, the trainer should say, 'Whoa!' followed by 'Good' for the horse's compliance to this simple command. The trainer should then advance steadily towards the horse, coiling the lunge rein into his left hand as he goes. When he reaches the horse's head he should take up his position on the horse's right side and walk him forward to the middle of the circle. If the horse has faced the trainer and then pulled backwards, the trainer can use this movement to his own advantage by saying 'Back!' and following this by his persistent backing right round the school because no horse enjoys going backwards for an appreciable distance. When the lunger feels that the horse is fed up with going backwards and is wanting genuinely to go forwards again he should say 'Whoa!' firmly and stand still himself in the very instant when the horse halts and he should approach as before and reward the horse for halting. After a short pause, standing still, the trainer should lead the horse forward from the right or off side to the centre of the circle.

The next few seconds are extremely crucial. It is imperative that the lungeing area is completely free from all distractions and that the trainer is quick-witted, skilled and dexterous, and that he anticipates and parries every contra thought and action the horse may contemplate. Above all he must establish and maintain the strongest possible governing rapport with the horse's mind. The horse may have the stronger body but the trainer has the stronger will and superior reasoning ability.

Having led the horse forward to the middle of the circle the trainer should lead him in hand on a small circle around its centre-point. While so walking he should take his furled whip carefully into his left hand and urge the horse forward with small taps of his whip on the horse's right side. If the horse responds by offering to trot on the small circle, the trainer should praise him and allow him to trot on and to move out onto a larger circle track at an active trot.

Usually this will restore obedience but the trainer must be on his guard against further signs of nappiness. He will be justified and correct if he administers a well-measured sting-hit to keep the horse trotting actively if he shows any inclination to resort to his former nappy habit.

Although the above method will overcome nappiness on the lunge in the majority of cases, often trainers will be asked to help with mature, hardened sinners who have become artists in the skills of nap. For this work the trainer will need at least one trained assistant and he himself must be very adept at using long-reins.

First the horse should be lunged for 20 minutes in the direction he favours. He should be worked in all three gaits with a good active trot being the prime objective. Next, the trainer should him through stages 2, 3 and 4 of the British method of long-reining (see pages 116–20). All of this work should be continued on the favoured rein, preferably without any confrontation.

When all of this work has been completed satisfactorily, the trainer should ask his assistant to join him by the horse's head as he is halted on a small circle track. The trainer should ask the horse to make a short turn on the forehand and halt. The assistant threads a slip rein through the outer ring of the cavesson and leads the horse forward for a few steps in the new direction before halting and rewarding the horse. This procedure should be repeated several times with the assistant taking the more active part. It is best to call it a day at this point, to reward the horse and put him away in his loose box where he can digest the lesson.

The whole process should be repeated the next day and the assistant should lead the horse forward at trot for a few strides before halting and rewarding him. If there has been no body-language signifying resistance to working on the difficult rein, the trainer and his assistant should plan the best time for the assistant to slip the leading rein off during a trot and run forward at a tangent away from the horse. The trainer should be able to long-rein the horse perfectly normally on the less-favoured rein.

The third day's work should consist of a repetition of the second day and by the end of the fourth day the trainer should be able to work the horse equally in both directions with three or four changes of rein whilst in the fourth stage of long-reining. By the end of the week the trainer should be able to lunge the horse on a single lunge rein in either direction without any difficulty. No one else should lunge the horse for at least another week; thereafter the trainer should keep a watchful eye on him and be ready to take over at the first sign of any misdemeanour.

## REMINDERS

◆ Do remember the training code for the horse:

RAPPORT – UNDERSTANDING – CONFIDENCE – GOOD MANNERS – *REWARD*
PRACTICE – MENTAL AND PHYSICAL DEVELOPMENT – MORE *REWARD*.

◆ Do ensure that you make a strong link-up with the young horse's brain before you embark on every work session; and that you keep that link-up safe and secure throughout each lesson. The quality of the rapport between the trainer and the horse is of the utmost importance in every horse's training.

◆ Do be sure to have a good and experienced assistant present throughout all the early stages unless you are outstandingly expert and experienced.

◆ Do be quick-thinking, quiet, calm and firm.

◆ Do allow the horse to sniff and inspect each new piece of equipment before it is put on to him.

◆ Do make sure that you are in a safe place, i.e. an indoor school, or a high-ceilinged disused cattle-shed.

◆ Do remember to have reward at hand and to give it to the horse whenever it is deserved.

◆ Do make sure that the horse is quiet to lead about to either hand, in company with other horses and on his own, and in a variety of environments, so that his confidence is building up daily with regard to motorized vehicles and other strange sights and sounds.

◆ Do get the horse used to seeing you standing up on a box or a straw bale so that he is not frightened by seeing you on a higher plane than ground level. Unlike human beings, horses' eyes are set more to the side of their heads to enable them to see predators approaching from the rear; they can see behind them. Do remember that young horses are often alarmed when they see somebody sitting up on their backs for the first time.

◆ Do lunge the horse with tightened girths and with the stirrups hanging down for a day or two before you ride him; make sure they are not so long that they bang on and hurt his elbows. Always remember to put the stirrups up again before you walk him about outside on a hard surface. I have known of several horses who have suffered fatal injuries from falling over onto a hanging stirrup iron – broken ribs, punctured lung = dead horse.

◆ Do watch the horse and his reactions with great care and analyse his thoughts and feelings throughout all his work. Give him time to develop confidence.

◆ Do accustom the horse to having a human body leaning on and then hanging across his back just behind the withers. The more a young horse can learn to trust the human being as he does these extraordinary things on and around him before he is actually backed, the better. If this training is done well, backing will be no problem.

◆ Do keep vigilant. If the young horse shows any sign of nervousness or resentment it is as well to call on 'George' to stand in for the rider. It is unfair and foolish to try to rush the horse; it is far better to lunge him with the stirrups hanging down and then with 'George' on his back for a day or two before you carry on with backing and riding him.

## WARNINGS

◆ Do not ever mount up on a young, green horse until he knows you and the prepara-tory work, and he is in a quiet mood and you have at least one experienced assistant to help you.

◆ Do not ever mount any horse when he is tied up in his stable.

◆ Do not try to back a young horse if you are in a hurry or nervous; if your nerve is in question or you suffer from old injuries it is better to ask a good lightweight rider to be your assistant and to do the mounting while you hold and discipline the young horse.

◆ Do not get your horse too fit with the lungeing work before you back him or he may emulate the wolf in Little Red Riding Hood and say of his bulging muscles, 'All the better to buck you off, my dear!'

# 9

# *Lungeing over Fences*

Although the task of lungeing horses over fences may appear to be simple, that is far from the truth. A great deal of trained skill is required if the results are to be beneficial rather than disastrous.

## Advantages of lungeing a horse over a fence

1. It develops the horse's technique and confidence, teaching him how to think and coordinate his brain, his limbs and his body as he is encouraged to jump over obstacles in the easiest possible way, without a rider-burden on his back.

2. It improves the horse's form on the flat as well as over poles and fences by loosening him up and encouraging him to make better use of his head, neck, back and limbs, encouraging him to be a better athlete.

3. It builds up his confidence by developing his technique for a rider-sport which is not in fact a natural activity for a horse. In the wild, horses and ponies are grazing creatures of the plains and of moorland.

4. As his confidence grows, the horse has time to discover and understand the existence of take-off zones. He cannot attend a lecture on the subject, so he has to learn about this in a practical way for himself. As the horse's knowledge and judgement of take-off zones improves, his confidence and his physical skill will develop. He will learn to raise the front of his trunk so that he makes room for his hind legs to come forward under the mass of his body-weight to produce the power and thrust from the ground. At the same time his fore limbs are freed to fold up neatly as he lifts his forehand into the air for lift-off.

5. It increases the horse's interest in his work by introducing elements of variety, achievement and fun into the lesson plans.

6. Using the additional verve created by the horse's enjoyment of the work, it improves the quality of his trot and canter gaits on the flat after one or two jumps.

7. The variety of the work over a few different types of fences stimulates interest and brain training.

These objectives can only be gained if the quality of the lunger's work is good enough; he must be sufficiently expert with his technique and he must gain experience by supervised practice with many horses – trained horses first, and then young horses and ponies. This can be a fascinating facet of horse training, but the results can be quite calamitous if the lunger's natural quickness, feel, talent and standard of training are insufficient.

## Learning to lunge horses and ponies over fences

Before any work of this nature is embarked upon, the lunger should remove the side reins. Whether the horse wears a well-padded roller, breaststrap and crupper, or whether he wears nothing at all, is purely up to the lunger. Both dressed and undressed versions are equally good from the horse's point of view.

The handling of the equipment has been explained in Chapter 4 and for the lunger's own safety those correct techniques must be implemented to the letter whenever he is lungeing a horse over fences. The rein must be coiled correctly in the rein (leading) hand, and the whip must be held in the whip (following) hand. The lunger has to be extremely dexterous and agile, with speedy yet stable footwork, in order to lunge a horse or pony well over a pole or a fence. He must always be in the right place at the right moment. He should remember that the blackest marks he can get are if he causes a horse to refuse to jump a fence by frightening or overfacing him; or if he puts off the horse by either moving too quickly ahead of him, or being too slow minded and slow footed to be able to inspire the horse forward over the fence. A good lunger will use a nice measure of his leading as well as driving influences.

The technique of using circle and straight-line tracks in order to position the horse's approach to the fence accurately must be perfected over ground-poles before any lunger attempts to put a horse over a fence on the lunge.

The skill whereby the lunger always brings the horse into the approach to the fence on a track which is exactly at a right-angle to the fence should be so well ingrained in the horse's mind that he can rely on instinctive timing and precision.

The lunger must build low fences which are suitable for the purpose; which means that the fence should be acceptable, educational and inviting to the horse. The lunge-rein must be guided over the side of the fence by a smooth pole, placed at just the right angle from the approach side and giving the lunge-rein a clear run over the highest projection of the fence itself, i.e. the nearest wing or fence support.

It is imperative that the lunger allows the horse to have complete freedom of his head and neck for the stride before the fence, over it, and after landing, and that a soft contact is regained swiftly yet smoothly afterwards.

The lunger must be aware that often the act of leaping can make the horse feel very exuberant and he must be ready to apply a strong restraint immediately after the horse has made good his landing. Remember to adopt the special technique for holding an obstreperous horse described on pages 42–4, if necessary.

As the horse progresses to jumping fences as opposed to a ground-pole or a low cross-pole fence, the lunger should remember that a fence with a slight spread is always easier for a horse to judge. It encourages the horse to arc over the fence with a good bascule as he jumps, and is more inviting than is an upright type of fence.

The lunger should change the rein at regular intervals – and he must be sure to re-arrange the fence accordingly.

*After the horse has been walked and trotted between empty uprights, a ground-pole may be laid between them and then a low cross-pole may be introduced. Don't forget to move the guiding/sliding pole.*

Finally, *reward* – don't forget it and do be generous with both praise and titbits.

### Training the young horse to jump

*Preliminary work*

As jumping is not a natural exercise for a horse he needs to be taught how to organize his limbs and develop dexterous footwork, balance and coordination in order to be proficient at leaping over fences. A horse can only be a bold jumper if he is confident in his own ability and has been encouraged to enjoy jumping by spontaneous praise and quick reward. No horse should be asked to jump fences until he has attained a good standard in his lungeing work and is sufficiently fit.

Before the lunger attempts to lunge a young horse even over a pole on the ground, he should have gained the horse's confidence by leading him, from either side, over undulating ground, small dips, low banks, even over very low tree trunks, gradually increasing the demand until the horse will follow his trainer by his side, wherever the latter is able to jump on his own two feet. Ditches should be included in this itinerary and the horse should be rewarded generously on the landing side of each small obstacle. It is obvious that the better the agility of the lunger, the better trained will be the horse! The trainer must always be aware of the dangers which could accompany this exercise; it would be quite easy to be kicked or jumped upon by mistake, or on purpose.

## Lungeing over ground-poles

It is easiest for the horse to understand this work if the trainer puts out one ground-pole in the usual enclosed lungeing area which has good, level footing. The pole should be just inside or outside the large circle track, whichever is most convenient.

The lunger should introduce the pole by leading the horse over it in hand, with a coiled lunge-rein, in each direction. Then he will find it easy to regulate the horse's circling at trot so that he directs the horse straight over the middle of the ground-pole as often as he intends. He must be guided by the natural calmness, balance and gait of the horse and only put him over the pole when all these qualities are in place.

There is a slight risk when working a horse over ground-poles that he might knock the back of his feet or the underside of a fetlock joint on the pole if he does not go over it in a straight and balanced manner. There are vulnerable bones and tissues in both of these places, i.e. pedal and navicular bones in the foot, and sesamoid bones, ligaments and flexor tendons under and at the back of the fetlock joint. One further word of warning that applies to all ground-poles: under no circumstances should a horse ever be allowed to catch the front of his foot on

*Ground-poles add interest to the lunge lesson as well as improving the engagement of the hindlegs and the quality of the gaits.*

*Here a trainer is making excellent use of a corner of the sand arena. The young horse jumps the placing pole and low fence in good style.*

the end of a ground-pole which he is approaching end-on, for from that angle a heavy pole is totally static, and the jarring to the foot and the leg can be extremely and permanently damaging.

When the horse is thoroughly confident about trotting over a single ground-pole, and if the lungeing area is large enough, several single poles can be placed around the area for the horse to be lunged over one at a time. Next he can be worked over two or three poles, well spaced out, with their centres set at 2.4–3 m (7–11½ ft) apart, on a fan-shape. Horses enjoy this work, and it is very beneficial in improving their trot gaits; further poles can be added on the same circle track, as required, and the distances can be closed to 1.2–1.5 m (3¾–4 ft) when the horse is confident.

The advantage of the fan-shape is that by increasing the diameter of the track over the poles, the lunger can ask for more engagement and longer strides where the far ends of the poles are wider apart. The trainer must be diligent and make frequent pole adjustments to suit each individual horse's way of going in that day's lesson. Rarely are any two horses, or any two days' work, identical. Lungeing a fit and relatively experienced horse at canter over single poles will often improve the quality of his canter.

*Lungeing over a single fence*

The selection of the site and the construction of the fence are extremely important.

The site should be outside the diameter of the large circle, for instance on the outer track at C or A, so that the wall of the school or lunge area helps the horse to

*He then has a good look at what is to come . . .*

*. . . and jumps the small spread fence well. Note the harmony of the trainer's aids and his agility, perfectly matching the horse's needs.*

*a Trainer and horse enjoying themselves on the cross-country course.*

*b It is always fascinating to watch the horse combine mental and physical powers.*

*c This trainer is a star rider across country, which is a distinct advantage.*

a

keep his balance as he works from and to the circle track. This is the easiest place for the horse to be started in this phase of his training as there will only be a very short distance of straight track, by A or C, and the wall ahead will encourage him to stay calm and to land with his inside legs leading, which is good for his training as well as being safest for his mind and his legs.

For the fence it is best to use a heavily built pair of uprights; they should be approximately 75 cm (2½ ft) in height; a sliding pole must always be placed on the topmost point of the inner upright. This pole has two objectives: it invites the horse to go through the gap between the uprights and it ensures that the lunge-rein slides smoothly over the fence without any part of the fence catching or interfering with the rein and the horse's head, and it accustoms

the horse to this action of the lunge-rein which he will not have encountered before.

It is wise to lunge the horse between empty uprights before putting a ground-pole between them. It is very natural for a horse to be suspicious of anything that might be regarded as a trap, and a raised pole straight ahead with another raised pole almost at right angles by its side can look very like a trap.

Progression from the ground-pole to a cross-pole fence, which encourages the horse to jump in the centre of the fence, and thence to a variety of different constructions is quite easy providing the lunger has a fairly good imagination.

The lunger must always remember to change the sliding pole to the other side of

110

b

c

the inner upright whenever he changes the rein on which he is working the horse over the fence.

The fence should never be too high. The lunger should aim to develop the young horse's *confidence* and his *style* – a good bascule is much more important than attempting a Herculean task.

### Lungeing over more than one fence at a time

There are two main options for this phase. The trainer can set out two or more individual fences on opposite sides of the lungeing area or he can build a 'double' of two small fences set for one non-jumping stride between them. Later the combination can be closed up to a 3–4 m (10–13 ft) distance, i.e. without a non-jumping stride between them, to form a low bounce fence.

These three combinations of fences should only be attempted by lungers who are fit and who can run like the proverbial hare. It is imperative that the lunger is fleet of mind and foot in order that he may allow the horse freedom of his head and neck from the moment of take-off at the first fence until after he lands over the second (or following) fences.

### Problem horses

Owing to the fact that jumping is not a natural activity for horses, invariably problems will arise. The most common ones are that the horse develops a habit of refusing or running out; or his jumping technique is poor and therefore his performance is disappointing.

The causes for both these dilemmas are often interrelated:

- Bad lungeing and/or riding mentally: lack of nerve or negative thinking on the lunger's or rider's part, such as, 'I don't think he'll like this fence,' or worse, 'I'm sure he is going to stop!'; too much bravado which overrules common sense and horse consideration, overfacing the horse; lack of mental rhythm and rapport about the whole exercise.

- Bad riding physically: rider's weight out of balance; over-riding; under-riding; inconsistent contact of leg and rein aids; rider holding breath with a resultant tense stiffness inhibiting timing, balance and suppleness; catching the horse in the mouth at any phase of the jump; jumping higher than the horse; banging down on his back with a thud as the horse lands.

- Pain: he may have some hidden misalignment in his trunk or limbs which is not significant enough to show in his work on the flat. If, despite a reasonably progressive programme and generous rewards, the horse does not enjoy his jumping and even refuses, he should be checked over thoroughly from his shoes and feet upwards.

Providing they are sound, horses who are shy of jumping can all be helped to improve their confidence and performance by some skilled work over simple fences on the lunge. The fences may be adapted to help the horse's technique e.g., when he is confident over simple fences, a narrow length of soft, brightly coloured plastic laid at the bottom of the fence will encourage the horse to look and to bascule over the fence, as well as improving his confidence to trust his trainer and jump over fences that look *very* strange. The lunger must ensure that the plastic is not off-putting, and be determined that the horse *will* jump the fence. (Mental determination, not whip strength, please!)

A rider whose own riding faults are impairing his horse's performance over fences has to be cajoled into accepting help himself, rather than continuing to blame his horse for cowardice or disobedience. Sometimes a nervous pupil will request to have a jump lunge lesson. It is my experience that this should not be undertaken, as in practice it is too difficult an exercise for all concerned. The timing of the lunger's influence and the size of the circle inevitably combine to magnify the balance problem, and it is then quite impossible to get three minds and bodies exactly synchronized in their actions. It is far better for novice or nervous riders to have a simple lesson on the flat and over very low fences in a small, enclosed arena rather than on a lunge-rein.

# 10

# Long-reining

Long-reining is a fascinating subject in its own right. It is developed from lungeing skills but it is far more difficult to do well and there is a much greater risk of causing damage to the horse than there is with lungeing.

Long-reining may be carried out in a variety of ways, to suit the special circumstances of the horse and lunger concerned. I believe that all horsemen and women should be adept at working horses and ponies with long-reins.

For many decades long-reining has been the subject of much discussion, and even of heated arguments. There are two distinct camps. Those who approve and who use long-reins avow that they find them very useful; they admit that the technique is difficult, but they can produce many success stories, particularly concerning the reformation of spoiled and problem horses; they believe that with training and natural talent and with dedicated practical application, long-reining can be developed into an art. Those who disapprove of long-reining do so because they are worried, quite rightly, that if the person concerned lacks training and expertise, he or she may do irreparable damage to the horse, particularly to his mouth, his form and his gaits.

There are two methods of long-reining: the British method, which can be from the side and from behind, and the Swedish method where the reins work from a much higher position through the terrets or rings on the top of the roller, a position which is much nearer to that of the rider's hands. I have found both of these methods to be very useful. There is in fact another method, that used at the Spanish Riding School in Vienna, where the horse is worked on very short long-reins, close to and directly behind the horse's hind legs; even with top experts this method has proved to be dangerous.

As well as being fascinating, long-reining has many practical uses; at one end of the scale it is an excellent way of schooling children's ponies who are too small to be ridden by an adult, but whose training needs to be thorough and complete. Even the most wayward of ponies can be reformed into a well-mannered child's pony by this form of training.

All young horses and ponies will benefit from the inclusion of this work from time to time in their daily work programme, before they are ridden; it also enables the trainer to advance their understanding and obedience without their having to carry the weight of a rider-burden on their backs. The work aids muscular development, thereby improving the young horses' mental and physical ability to carry their riders for a little longer each day at the end of the lesson.

Older horses who have developed problems under saddle – usually caused by the person who sits on the saddle! – can be watched, worked and re-trained through skilful work on long-reins. If a trainer is unable to ride he can work any standard of horse to advantage and, if he has a well-trained riding horse, together they can develop long-reining into an art form.

The equipment that is required for long-reining varies slightly depending on the method used.

When the horse is worked with the long-reins attached to the bit, it is essential that the trainer is not only skilled but that he is particularly gifted with deft, light and sympathetic handling of the reins. Ponderous thoughts and heavy hands can destroy the horse's training and the whole of his future life.

## The British method

The positioning of the rings or the stirrups through which the reins pass is very important. The rings should be set on the roller midway between the top of the withers and the top of the elbow joint.

The four stages of the British method are as follows. For these training stages, the horse is worked mainly on a circle.

### Stage one

This stage is carried out in exactly the same

*The first stage of long-reining is exactly the same as for lungeing. Note the lunger has paid out half a loop as she encourages the horse to move out onto a bigger circle.*

115

manner as is used when training a young horse to lunge, until he has learned acceptance of the words of command for the transitions up and downward, to and from the three basic gaits, and to wear the training roller with its breastplate and crupper (see Chapter 7).

When the horse moves forward confidently, willingly and well to command then he can be moved on to stage two.

## Stage two

The second long-rein is now introduced; both reins being attached to the side rings at the front of the cavesson. The inside rein passes straight to the trainer's hand, while the outer rein is threaded through the highest of the outer side rings on the training roller, over the horse's back, immediately behind the top of the roller and thence back to the trainer's hand, which also carries the lunge-whip. The reins have to be re-arranged on the training roller before every change of rein.

The object of this stage is to introduce the second rein. Some young horses may be a bit worried when they first spy the second rein coming from a strange place on their back; most accept it quite readily. The trainer should choose his moment carefully to make little flapping movements with the outside rein – not to frighten the horse but rather to increase his confidence in its

*The British method of long-reining, stage two – the second rein is introduced.*

presence, and possibly as an aid to increase his impulsion. Thus he will be prepared for the next stage.

## Stage three

For this stage the inside rein passes straight to the trainer's hand as before, but now the time has come to introduce the outside rein in its final position: that is, around the outside of the horse's hind legs. This has to be done with great care in order to avoid causing any upset to the horse. While the horse is standing still the trainer keeps a firm hold on the inner, direct rein – under no circumstances must he let go of it. He then adjusts the outer rein so that it runs straight back from the cavesson to the middle or lowest ring on the roller. From the roller the rein should be fairly slack to the top of the croup where the trainer will place two or three loops, carefully folded on top of each other, just behind the sacroiliac ridge or 'jumping bump'. There is quite a knack in adjusting the rein and its loops to stay in place while the horse

*The British method, stage three – the outer rein is being introduced. Three loops of the rein are in position on the top of the horse's croup, ready to slide down as the horse walks forward.*

walks forward. Care must be taken that the horse is not kept standing for too long and that the rein does not fall down either prematurely or suddenly.

The trainer should tell the horse positively to 'Walk on' as he holds the remainder of that rein in his outer hand held at shoulder height, in order that the rein may glide back over the horse's quarters as he walks forward. The trainer should then tell the horse to 'Trot on' while keeping a normal, consistent yet soft contact with the direct inner rein and an almost non-existent contact with the outer rein, which should hang softly at just below hock level as the horse trots quietly around the trainer.

As horses tend to vary greatly in their character and in their acceptance of what we wish and expect them to do, all may not go according to plan as described above. Occasionally a nervous horse may leap forwards, away from the snake-like thing on his back, and take off as fast as he can 'leg-it' around the trainer. If this should happen, the lunger should change his stance immediately, he must *keep calm* and hold on to the direct rein firmly, adopting the strong position with the rein hand on his hip and the opposite leg braced towards the horse's forehand.

The voice should be used to calm and reassure the horse – there is no point in trying to tell him to slow down, as he will not listen and he will learn to disobey rather than to obey. When horses panic they hold their breath and this reaction, combined with the physical effort of skirmishing around the trainer, will soon result in the horse developing a natural desire to slow down of his own accord. He should be

a

b

*a As Cavalier trots forward the outer rein slides down. It is very important to allow it to lie loosely.*

*b Cavalier realizes there is something new about all this and gets very impulsive, too fast for his own balance.*

*c The new procedure is accepted and he makes a fluent transition to the gait of walk.*

told to 'Trot on' with good, bold strides while he absorbs the fact that the second rein is still there, around his hocks, and that it is not at all harmful, or even uncomfortable. Next the horse can be slowed down, praised, then halted and given his reward before the reins are re-adjusted as above, after which he can be re-started very carefully to work in the other direction.

Another common entangling problem which a trainer may encounter when he is new to this form of work is that he may not allow the outer rein to be free enough to slide quietly from the croup to hock level. If he keeps any sort of a pull on the outer rein, it can get itself tucked up under the horse's dock. This has a galvanizing effect on the horse who will clamp down his tail over the rein and rush around, kicking up with both hind legs as he goes. Should this occur, the trainer should play out the rein so that it drops down onto his hocks, and its weight will then pull the rein from under the tail. As long as there is nothing within a radius of 30 m (98 ft) on which a loose rein might get entangled, it is best to release the outer rein and allow it to swing out and follow the horse; from this position it will soon fall free and order may be restored quite quickly.

Hopefully the third stage will have been completed in a calm and uneventful manner, and the horse will have gained in confidence, strength and in responsiveness to the trainer's aids.

c

## Stage four

This is the final stage of the British method of long-reining and is a natural progression from the preceding three stages. After the horse has worked calmly and well in his lungeing and long-reining lessons up to and including stage three, the trainer can introduce stage four. The work is much more difficult and therefore the trainer needs to be highly skilled in the art of long-reining or he could damage the horse by rough rein aids or by asking too much of him for too long.

When the trainer decides that the horse is ready for stage four, having worked him for ten to twenty minutes through the first and third stages as a revision and a preparation for the fourth stage, he will call the horse to a halt. The reins are still fastened to the rings on each side of the front of the cavesson, not to the bit.

The inner rein is now threaded through the ring which is at the middle height, on the inner side of the training roller, rather than running directly to the trainer's hand. The outer rein should also go through the middle ring to match the inner one. This rein placement allows the trainer to work the horse on each rein or to either hand, without any interrupting pauses.

Due to the inner rein's new position, running through the ring on the roller, the trainer should work from a position which is slightly further back i.e., behind the girth rather than behind the point of the shoulder, so that he is related to the reins moving from his hands to the roller. He will now be able to teach his horse to understand the rein aids and to follow their soft guidance.

By sensible use of more frequent changes of rein at walk and later at trot, the trainer can accustom the horse to making quick yet fluent adjustments to his body-weight,

*In the British method, both reins go through the rings on the roller. This means that the horse may be worked in both directions without any interrupting adjustments. Cavalier has found self-carriage.*

his balance, his coordination and to the dexterity of his footwork with no change to the rhythm of the walk or trot gaits.

These changes of rein must always be carried out very smoothly to avoid any risk of upsetting the horse's confidence or straining his joints, ligaments or tendons. The work will prepare him for similar work when he is ridden.

This fourth stage is particularly useful for schooling children's ponies and for re-schooling horses who, due to a poor standard of training, have lost their confidence or have developed bad habits.

It is also possible to develop this fourth-stage work to include more advanced dressage movements up to and including lateral work, flying changes, piaffe and passage, which is quite useful for spectacular demonstrations. My personal preference is to ride these movements as I have never found it easy to get sufficient impulsion, roundness, engagement and cadence from the more 'remote control' method of long-reining.

When the horse has reached the fourth stage, with a long-rein on each side of the horse's body and the reins running through rings on the roller or stirrups on the saddle, the trainer may work the horse from two alternative positions. When using stirrups, they should be adjusted so that the tread of the iron is level with the bottom edge of the saddle flap, and then tied together under the horse's chest with a short piece of cord which lies on the girth.

The trainer may work the horse from the side as for lungeing, as just described – this method is particularly useful for horses who have learned how to be evasive, or downright disobedient, due to bad training. Alternatively the trainer may drive the horse from behind – this position is extremely useful to give a young horse confidence and courage to go forward on his own, with his two-legged friend directing him.

It is best to start young horses using the side rings of the cavesson rather than the bit for either of these positions. It is also wisest at first to start in an enclosed manège. If you attempt to train your young horse on open farmland, the unexpected might set him off and introduce you to some high-class land-skiing. The bit is a necessary form of control for the great outdoors.

By using the alternative position the trainer can drive the young horse forward to explore the surrounding fields, bridle-ways or moors. This teaches the horse to go on ahead, virtually by himself (not quite, of course). He learns to gain in confidence as he is driven forward through strange surroundings and over varied terrain. This

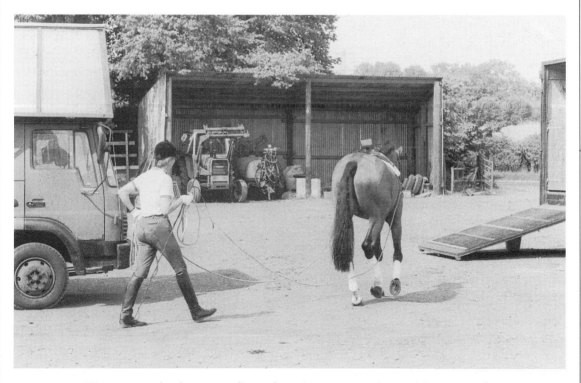

*However spooky the surroundings, the trainer must retain a positive approach.*

121

*The British method of changing the rein and thus direction from right to left.*

*a 'Goodness, do you REALLY mean me to turn OUTwards?'*

*b 'This does seem to be a very strange idea.'*

*c 'I think you're crazy, but I'll do it.'*

*d 'I see – it was all incredibly easy after all!'*

a

b

c

d

a                                                                                                                    b

*The Swedish method of changing from the right rein.*                          *To the left – engaging*

is good fitting work for horse and trainer. If the trainer is sufficiently experienced in this work he may include low, natural obstacles in his walk-about; he must be sure to allow the horse complete freedom of his head and neck as he negotiates difficult footing and any obstacles.

Unfortunately in many urban areas speedy traffic has put an end to leisurely ambles around country lanes which used to be a most pleasurable exercise for horse and trainer. At the British Cavalry School at Weedon the young horses were long-reined from behind over the permanent fences of hedges and banks on a hundred acres of farmland; certainly their trainers were very fit and agile!

## The Swedish method

The trainer long-reins the horse with the reins running through the terrets on the top of a driving saddle. Both the British method, on circles, and the Swedish method are for horses who are at least trained to understand how to follow guidance from a soft, smooth rein aid.

In the Swedish method the trainer works alongside the horse, who is already trained to work on the lunge. The trainer uses circles, straight lines and many fluent changes of rein in order to help the horse to establish a better form for himself, by encouraging his natural forward urge whilst improving his balance, his looseness and suppleness and his coordination.

124

c

*hindlegs. . .*                    *. . . and canter*

Lateral work can be included when the horse is being worked both on circles and in straight lines. This is not usually carried beyond the preliminary exercise of leg yielding at walk and later at trot. The presence of the two reins helps the horse's understanding of the trainer's request that he should move forward and sideways, keeping his body as straight as the track dictates and in each case having an almost imperceptible flexion of his poll, away from the direction of the movement.

Leg yielding is an invaluable exercise for removing excess tension, and for introducing lateral work before the young horse is ready mentally or physically to be asked for the collection and bending required in the more advanced lateral work. It is also a most important exercise for developing the adductor and abductor muscles of the young horse's trunk, i.e. the muscles which bring the limbs in towards the trunk and those which take the limbs away from the trunk. By developing these weight-carrying muscles, the trainer gives the horse some easy but very effective body-building exercises. These in turn make it easier for him to support and to carry the weight of his rider and to move with freedom and with grace under that weight.

### To change the rein when working a horse on long-reins

This can be done in either the British or

the Swedish methods of long-reining but trainers must remember that in the British method it is only possible to change the rein on the move in stage four.

Although lungers should be taught this manoeuvre from the halt it is easier for the young horse to understand, learn and accomplish, if he is kept moving forward in the gait of walk.

The trainer drives the horse along a circle track which is approximately 6 m (20 ft) from the school wall. On the left rein, as the horse walks along the trainer takes his whip and both reins into his left hand; he then slides his right hand as far as he can reach along the right rein towards the horse without exerting any pressure on that rein. As the horse approaches the designated spot, when his body is parallel with the school wall, the trainer applies a steady but very soft pull on the right rein. As soon as the horse begins to respond by turning outwards towards the wall, the trainer allows the left rein to slide out smoothly and swiftly through the fingers of his left hand.

The presence of the wall teaches the horse to improve his balance on to his hindquarters and, as he completes the turn and returns to the circle track on the right rein, the trainer should urge him forward into a good working trot.

Although the new outside rein must be paid out freely, its usefulness in regulating the end of the turn must be remembered to assist the horse to balance and work off his inside hind leg; he should not be allowed to over-turn and fall on to his forehand with the front of his trunk dropped down between his shoulder-blades, or much of the good of the gymnastic work will have been lost.

As soon as the horse is confident at making these changes of rein at walk, they can be practised at trot, and the horse will soon offer the changes of direction from the commands of his trainer's thoughts, body language and voice alone. These changes of rein are one of the finest exercises for relaxing a tense horse and for improving every horse's confidence, suppleness, balance and, in fact, the whole of his form.

# *Lunge Lessons for the Rider*

Most equestrian experts agree that lunge lessons are beneficial to riders of every standard, ranging from the beginner to those who have reached an advanced level of competence.

First, 'Get the aim straight!' The main objective of a lunge lesson for you, the rider, is to help you to understand the correct riding skills to a greater depth. Lunge lessons will also improve your fitness and, providing the instructor is well trained, they will ensure that you develop a feel and competence for analysing which muscles you should use, as well as why and how you should use

*A lunge lesson helps with the formation of a new partnership. Here the rider is getting to know a new and bigger pony, with both partners concentrating on each other.*

them. By developing your knowledge and awareness, your posture and confidence will improve in the speediest as well as in the most natural way.

## Advantages for the rider

1. On the lunge, you are probably as safe as you can be when riding a horse due to the fact that the horse's behaviour, gait and speed are all controlled by an experienced horseman or woman, at the other end of the lunge-rein.

2. The one-to-one aspect is heightened by the very close proximity of the lunger to the rider and the horse – they are virtually all tied together by the lunge-rein.

3. Your posture and aid application can be improved by suggestion, appreciation, correction, encouragement and earned praise.

4. The lunger can instil confidence in a rider who is by nature apprehensive. If you have a horse of your own, this facet of your education can be doubled if your horse is worked on the lunge first without a rider and then with an experienced rider on his back to improve the horse's confidence.

You should watch the horse while he is receiving his share of the education, as it is too good an opportunity to watch his movement and reactions to be missed.

Some riders are too diffident to ask if they may watch, so it is up to the lunger to ensure that they do receive a friendly invitation to do so.

5. Similarly, the same pattern of work should be followed if a rider asks for help with a horse who has a problem; although in this case, it will probably be better if the rider has a lesson on an experienced and reliable lunge horse while his or her own horse is lunged separately by an experienced trainer. Thus rider and horse will be learning how to ride and move better respectively, before working together.

6. Providing that the lunger is a trained instructor, he can introduce you to the value, strength and 'magic' of the thought aid – the rapport between rider and horse. In my experience all too few riders have learned how to use this aid to the maximum enjoyment of both members of the horse-and-rider partnership. It is, after all, the first of the six natural aids:

1. Thought
2. Weight
3. Legs
4. Rein aids
5. Voice
6. Mental and physical *feel*

It is essential that all six natural aids are taught by the instructor and that he helps you to grasp a true and deeper understanding of each one in every subsequent lesson.

7. Due to his proximity, the instructor can soon give you a real understanding of how to establish a supple, steady seat; by which I mean that you learn how to sit well, from the soles of your feet up through your body and limbs to the top of your head. The main aim is to be as easy a rider-burden as possible for the horse to carry. (The main aim should never be merely to 'look good'.)

8. With a good instructor, lunge lessons should help you to achieve a proper understanding of and feel for sitting in harmony with the balance and movement of the horse, with every part of your body.

*Due to centrifugal force, riders' bottoms slide outwards. The rider loses balance and poise, treading on the outside stirrup and leaning inwards with the elbows and upper arms springing away from her body — not very easy for the horse.*

a

*Two more subtle faults — the rider's eyes have lost contact with the horse's brain stem at the poll and her inside leg is much too far back, pushing the hindquarters out rather than asking for a soft bending around the rider's inside leg positioned at the girth.*

b

9. Lunge lessons should help you to develop your analytical powers and to feel for the rhythm which suits the horse exactly and for a good quality in the muscle work of the horse's back under your seat.

10. You should strive to attain perfect longitudinal and lateral balance at all times, and particularly when you are riding increase and decrease of circles and transitions.

11. As you achieve equestrian balance by making smooth yet precise shifts of your seat bones to the inside of a curving track, you can feel how you have enabled the horse to move with an optimum of ease, grace and vigour under the correctly balanced rider-burden.

To me this is logical common sense, yet not all instructors are prepared to accept and teach this simple truth. Instead they allow their pupils to slide outwards, to sit crookedly and to blame their horses.

Unless riders understand and achieve these last six simple yet deeper fundamental facts, they will never be able to think for and with their horses or to make subtle shifts of their weight to guide and influence their horses in an easy, unobtrusive yet effective way.

Riders should be encouraged to take their own time (not *too* much of it!) to discover how regular and thoughtful practising of all these techniques will enable them to ride their horses through smooth transitions, within and between gaits, through changes of direction, and between different school movements, all with invisible aids. Surely this must be the goal for which all dedicated riders wish to strive?

## EXERCISES FOR RIDERS DURING LUNGE LESSONS

Good exercises are those which are designed to meet the needs of each individual rider, tactfully to correct any faults which cause unwanted stiffness or lack of the desired levels of balance, coordination and harmony, but those that are described on pages 131–140 provide a good set of general exercises beneficial to most riders.

Although the exercises themselves may be absolutely correct in their concept and in their content, they will be valueless or even dangerous if they are not performed properly. So it is important that each exercise is introduced at the halt, and the instructor describes its purpose as well as checking that each rider has got it exactly right.

I must stress that any exercise that jerks or hurts should be avoided as they can cause chronic injury to a rider's joints, ligaments, tendons and/or muscles. See page 142 for the sort of exercises to avoid.

### For the instructor

As a general rule, all physical exercises should be explained, demonstrated and discussed while the horse and rider are standing square and still and whilst there is no movement to distract them from these vital introductions.

The instructor must have sufficient belief in the value of these exercises to practise them himself when he is riding and to return to their use frequently in all the lessons he gives, to pupils of every standard. The positive feed-back from pupils which invariably follows a run-through of some of the following exercises never fails to thrill and reassure me.

At the commencement of every lesson it is essential that the instructor makes an up-to-date assessment of the pupil's present standard of competence in order that he may adapt his lesson plan to suit the pupil's requirements for that day.

A newly qualified and therefore comparatively inexperienced instructor will often spoil what could have been a *good* lunge lesson by trying to make it too 'active'. In fact, they then risk making the 'activity' annihilate the time needed for thinking, for analysing, for experimenting with various adjustments and resultant feels, and the time to *learn*.

As he watches he should take the opportunity to note whether the pupil is sitting in the centre of the saddle rather than on the back of it and then wait until the pupil has had his say. After taking careful note of the rider's ideas, if he deems it is necessary, the instructor should discuss the merits of his pupil's saddle and its fitting and balance.

If the rider seems to be waging a constant war against the effects of a too-low rear end of the saddle's seat, the instructor should ask him to stand up in his stirrups. While his weight is lifted from the saddle, the instructor should slide his whole hand under the back part of the saddle seat, just where the rider should sit, before he tells the rider to lower himself softly into the saddle again, with the instructor's hand and wrist underneath.

Usually the rider's face will instantly portray a very clear message of astonish-ment mixed with relief and delight, as he realizes that his riding faults cannot all be laid at his own door and that a little extra stuffing in the back of his saddle would make a real difference to the balance of his seat and to the effectiveness of his aids. He should be lent a correctly built and stuffed saddle for his lunge lesson as the lesson would be useless if he were to continue with his own saddle in its present state.

### Remember the lunge horse

I often think that if I were a lunge horse I could easily come to regard my job as a fairly ghastly occupation, being boring beyond measure, often very tiring and usually being extremely taxing to one's mind, joints and muscles.

I do not believe that it is necessary or right for the horse to make lunge lessons into a dreaded chore of endless medium-sized circles at a seemingly endless trot with a bumping, tiring and worsening rider-burden on his back. Rather, I believe that lunge lessons can and should be enjoyable, if not inspiring, to both the horse and the rider alike. However, all of this will depend on the prowess of the person in the middle, the lunger-instructor.

## A framework of good exercises

With the seat bones now established in the correct place, on the centre third of the saddle, start at the top.

### The nape of the neck exercises

There are three simple exercises the object of which is to lift and free the rider's head and neck:

1 Make several smooth but strong pulls upwards with the back of your head, as if you are trying to touch the sky or the roof of the indoor school, or as if the back of your head is attached to a star. Two additional mental pictures which can help are to think of growing tall ears, and to try to go on the bit – just as you ask your horse (or pony) to do, with direct flexions at the poll.

I hope you will have sufficient imagination to appreciate those two 'pictures' . . . I find that they often do turn the key of understanding.

You must guard against any tendency to be over-enthusiastic with this exercise. In point of fact; if the exercise is done correctly the head and nape of the neck 'pulls' should hardly show. Vigorous head-nodding and/or twisting is *not* what is required.

2. For the second exercise, make little circles in the air in front of you, with your nose, pulling the nape of your neck as long as you can as you do it.

3. The third exercise is similar to the second one, but instead of making little

*A good example of a pupil who is trying too hard at the beginning of a lesson. She is doing the exercise of stretching the muscles of the nape of the neck well, but there is too much excess tension in her lower back and hips.*

circles in the air, make a string of signs of infinity in the air (tiny figures-of-eight, lying on their sides).

Incidentally, these exercises are excellent means of dispersing stiffness and/or tiredness when driving long distances or coping with unexpected bouts of 'parking' on motorways! It is always good to practise good posture and, if carried out correctly, these exercises will not give rise to a battery of curious glances as, if they are well done, they are imperceptible.

### The shoulder-shrugging exercise

Raise the points of your shoulders up towards your ears. No cheating – the nape of your neck must stay stretched. Move them back, down, squeeze your ribs with the inner side of your upper arms and *hold*.

The objects of this exercise are to loosen the whole of the shoulder girdle, which riders often tense up without realizing what their shoulder muscles are up to! This exercise can open your eyes to many of the muscles you should use with subtle strength when you ride, and can help you understand how useful the back of the shoulder-blades are in assisting the influence of the rein aids which have their foundation there.

The muscle you can feel expanding on the rib-cage during the last part of this exercise is the latissimus dorsi muscle. This is the main trunk binding muscle. It has many interesting points of attachment like the base of the skull, the backs of the shoulder-blades, the tops of the hip bones, the rib-cage and inside the upper arm. It is easy to feel how this large muscle which lies on the outside of the rib-cage swells and strengthens when you *squeeze* and *hold*. The last attachment is the reason for the correction 'elbows in'.

### Stretching and easing the lower back exercise

This exercise involves leaning forward and sitting upright again, from the waist up, not from the hip joints.

As you ride forward at walk, make a smooth roll forwards with the upper part of your trunk, from your waist upwards, pull your tummy in and keep your pelvis upright. You will not be able to lean your shoulders forward very far. Imagine your horse is treading over a small ditch or a branch, placed at each circle point.

This exercise is an invaluable means of removing excess tension from your lower back; it will also help to improve the accuracy and technique of your riding of circles.

### The legs-away exercise

Lift the thighs and knees away and then lower them on to the saddle again. Repeat this exercise, slowly, gently and effortlessly, in your own time, finding a rhythm to suit you and your horse.

This exercise frees excess tension in your hip joints and gives you a real feel and awareness of where your seat-bones are. You will learn how your hips should move in easy synchronization with the movement of the horse's hind legs.

### The lower legs swinging exercise

Keeping your toes slightly raised, move one

*The first count of the shoulder-shrugging exercise.*

leg at a time 6–10 cm (2–4 in) backwards and squeeze your horse's rib-cage with it as you do so; rest that leg and repeat the exercise with the other leg, then work with both legs alternately in a slow-march time. Be careful not to set about your horse and confuse him with flailing legs; set your personal metronome to a really slow rhythm which suits your horse exactly.

This exercise will enable you to use your lower legs more steadily yet freely, and you will learn how to encourage the horse to make better use of his latissimus dorsi muscle. You will feel the effectiveness of this exercise in helping the horse to lift up the front of his trunk in the desired manner.

This exercise is especially helpful when ridden at a slow but active trot, and serves as a good preparation for horse and rider when you start to develop medium trot. It is also very helpful for young horses who have been asked to produce a stronger trot before their muscles are ready for such

*Knees and thighs away – an initial excess of enthusiasm made the feet join in as well!*

work on the whole of your leg, from your hip joint down to your toes, and think of rolling your thigh bones (femurs) over in front of the adductor and flexor muscles which lie inside and to the rear of your thighs so that they are no longer impeding the closeness of your thigh bones to the saddle.

It is always helpful if the instructor gives you a feel of this at the halt, by physically pulling the thigh muscles backwards from under the thigh bone, gently but firmly.

Instructors please note: beware of making too much of an issue of 'fat thighs' as it is easy to make pupils self-conscious and then they try too hard . . . or they do not try at all!

### Bending down to touch your inside toe with your inside hand

Take your reins and whip in your outside hand and let your inside hand hang down softly straight by your side vertical with the ground, just as it should be for a correct dressage salute.

Keeping your seat bones in place on the saddle, bend down to touch the toe of your boot and gently sit up again – down one, two up. Repeat several times before changing the rein and repeating the exercise with the other hand and toe.

This exercise is beneficial at walk and trot and may, with discretion, be ridden at canter. It is very helpful, not only for suppleness and agility, but also for the rider who has a problem in getting a feel for sitting in balance with the horse. The rider must not be over-taxed in the faster gaits.

work and who have learned to 'go wide behind' with weak, straddling hind legs. The slow timing of the rider's lower legs used alternately helps the horse to use his trunk muscles correctly and to move his hind legs along the same tracks as those of his front feet.

### Ankle and leg rolling

With your legs hanging down loosely, pull your toes up, in, down and rest. Try to

*Much good work has been done but excess tension causes stiffness in the pupil from time to time which, in turn, causes the horse to bend, drop the front of her trunk and overbend.*

### The stretching and deepening exercise

This exercise is done with the reins knotted. Start with both arms lowered and with lightly clenched hands hanging down vertical to the ground. Improve your posture – carry your head high. Key into your horse's brain. Uncurl the fingers and turn the palms of both hands forwards and outwards and upwards softly until they reach shoulder height. Hold it.

Stretch your upper body tall, pull up your head as high as it will go and stretch upwards as if lifting your seat bones off the saddle with the lightness you are giving yourself. Feel the added tension in the muscles of your pelvic girdle.

Now change – totally relax all the excess tension from your pelvic muscles. From your bottom rib downward – *slump*! Lower your arms, softly and slowly to retake their original position, hanging vertically down on either side. As you lower your arms, feel yourself sink down into the saddle; allow your two seat bones to feel the horse's back muscles, through the saddle. Yes, it *is* quite possible and this key must never be lost from your riding. You must keep asking yourself 'What is my horse thinking? How is he feeling – mentally and physically?' Try to sink softly through the saddle into a close contact with his back – no 'pushing', no 'shoving', no excess tension. Remember your posture, from the bottom rib upwards you should retain a supple and elegant poise. Preserve the new-found 'depth' of your seat.

When you have become accustomed to the feel of this exercise, you should add the 'nape-of-the-neck' exercises when your arms are outstretched, immediately after you have 'slumped'.

### Arm bending and stretching exercise

Starting with alternate arms, touch the point of your left shoulder with the tips of the fingers of your left hand, keeping your upper arm vertical and close to your body, and pull your shoulders straight. Straighten your arm softly and stretch it out to the side, parallel with the ground, and with the palm of the hand upwards with relaxed fingers. Repeat the exercise with the same hand slowly, several times, in rhythm with the four beats of the horse's walk. Bend on the first beat − hold it; stretch on the next first beat − hold. Then exchange hands and work the other arm for a few minutes in the same way.

The exercise may then be carried out at trot, again keeping the movements down to a slow speed.

Finally, if you feel safe and confident the instructor may suggest that you move on to the next stage, that of bending and stretching both arms simultaneously, first at walk and then at trot.

Remember, as with all exercises, to be very careful not to do too much for too long − there is always another day! Fatigued muscles ache for a long time afterwards and that can be most off-putting for future lunge lessons.

The instructor can give further helpful hints during ensuing lessons such as: try to time the bending and stretching so that you work with the rhythm of your horse's steps. At walk . . . bend − 1, 2, 3, 4, stretch − 1, 2, 3, 4, and so on. In other words, you hold each position for one complete stride.

At trot and at canter it is best if the instructor tells you to hold each position for two whole strides, to give you time to think and feel, and to feel and think, e.g. at trot . . . bend − 1, 2, 1, 2, stretch − 1, 2, 1, 2, and so on. At canter . . . 1, 2, 3 − 1, 2, 3 and 1, 2, 3, and so on.

Even as you read, the lunger (and the rider) can feel how helpful the counting aspect of these exercises is for the rider; never assume that a wonderful sense of rhythm sits inside every rider, for it does not! Many riders do not have much, if any, rhythm, but learning to ride well will help them to achieve a much better feeling for rhythm and will improve their coordination.

### Arm bending, trunk turning and arm stretching exercise

This exercise is an extension of the exercise described above. When you have your arms in the 'bent' position, turn your head and upper body round to the side. It is important that you keep your pelvis parallel with the horse's hips throughout the exercise; guard against being over-enthusiastic and turning your trunk too far as this causes an unwanted displacement of the hips.

It is easier and more natural to turn your upper body while your arms are bent, so you should have both arms bending, trunk

*The instructor has asked her pupil to ride to a square halt and to quit and cross her stirrups. Before they move forward, the pupil is introduced to the rein-giving exercise (see below).*

turning and arms stretching outwards, with the palms and fingers turned softly uppermost.

The instructor should lead you through the exact sequence of the exercise initially, but as soon as you have a feel for the movement and rhythm of the exercise, it is better to carry it out without interruption to your thought and feel.

### The rein-giving exercise

For this exercise, take up the reins. You may or may not have stirrups.

Forward with the right rein, moving the hand towards the horse's mouth, to make a loop in the rein. Softly take it back and re-establish a smooth, light contact. Forward with the left rein . . . and softly take it back . . . and repeat.

As soon as you have gained confidence and competence, work at the exercise in your own time. The instructor will assess the improvement in the form of both you and your horse.

This is an invaluable exercise for improving horses and riders. It is especially helpful to riders who have been badly taught and who have developed a steady, and heavy *pull* on both reins in the mistaken view that they have a contact, in a way which is most deadening to the horse's mouth and to his gaits.

Although, as with all exercises, this

exercise should be introduced at the halt and then the walk, its real benefits can be appreciated best whilst the horse is moving forward at a good working trot.

### The hand, wrist and elbow exercise

Keeping a soft contact throughout, smoothly raise the left hand, turning the thumb part slightly outwards as you raise it . . . and smoothly lower it again. Smoothly raise the right hand, turning the thumb part slightly outwards . . . and smoothly lower it again. Smoothly raise both hands, remember to turn the thumb part out slightly as you do so . . . and lower them again.

All exercises where the arms are lifted away from the body improve posture and muscle use if they are carried out with the palms of the hands uppermost. This turning makes the shoulder girdle control and support the upper limb so that its movements are softer and, at the same time, the muscles of the shoulder girdle are strengthened. A supine arm and hand position is always preferable, being better for a rider's posture, as is skipping with the skipping rope turning back over the head rather than the more common-place method of skipping with the rope being turned forward over the head, which rounds the shoulders, turns the elbows up and out and turns the backs of the hands uppermost . . . none of which habits make for good riding.

For those last two exercises the rider uses the reins. Sometimes for the last part of a lunge lesson the instructor may decide that it will be of greater benefit for a particular rider to have stirrups and reins while he is helped by the instructor and the lunge-rein to carry out some simple work such as smooth transitions within and between the gaits and any other simple school movements with which the rider may have a problem. This can be a very useful facet of some lunge lessons.

### Agility exercises

These can be helpful to encourage beginners to balance and to develop an independent seat, but I must add a word of warning about these exercises. They must only be carried out at the halt with responsible helpers holding the ponies' and horses' heads. If they are not held, a pony particularly will be very quick to grasp just when is the best moment to catch out his rider and may cause a child to be far more agile than was intended. When children are sufficiently confident and competent, then agility exercises can be very good for their senses of balance and of 'dash and dare' when carried out at walk, then trot. Many talented young riders will enjoy carrying out some of the exercises at canter too.

## Notes for the instructor:

It is very important that the instructor keeps a particularly watchful eye on his pupil's hips when he gives him arm exercises. Often when the rider concentrates on moving his arms about, he forgets to keep a check on the positioning of his hips and, unless he does think about this, his hips will move out of their correct alignment with the hips of the horse as he works under him on the lunge.

Due to the strong pull of centrifugal force when a horse is being lunged, all riders will have a natural tendency to slide out as

*A very interesting pupil. She used to ride her ponies with her lower leg too far forward. Now she has overdone the correction and is sitting out to the left with her inner leg too far back. These two faults have caused an unwanted forward tilt to the top of her pelvis. Her balance and seat improve as she moves her arms outwards.*

a

b

*The same pupil comes for another lesson. She is well in balance and her seat looks much more relaxed.*

they go round and round the lunger, especially when they are working at the stronger and faster gaits of trot and canter. Even a small slide is unfair to the horse but it can be quite difficult to see from the centre of the circle.

When the rider is not carrying out exercises to improve his balance, posture and suppleness, but has taken back his reins, the instructor must watch that he is sitting sufficiently to the inside, that his upper body is well-carried and vertical, that his inner hip is slightly forward and that at the same time, his inner shoulder is equally slightly backwards, so that the rider's hips are parallel with the horse's

hips and his shoulders are parallel with the horse's shoulders. Unless the rider develops this correct technique he will restrict his horse's potential as well as his gaits and the whole of his form.

The instructor must make regular 'spot checks' with regard to his pupil's sliding out, loss of balance and his consequent crookedness . . . and discomfort for the horse. He will find that the best solution is for him to enlist the aid of another skilled lunger who can lunge the pupil while the instructor teaches from outside the circle, where he can best see whether the rider's weight has been sufficiently shifted to the inside and that he keeps it there.

The instructor must also watch and analyse the rider's hips in another respect. If there is the slightest sign of his pupil's seat bones bumping together or as a pair on the saddle, he should call the rider to a halt and explain that when the horse trots he does not move his hind legs forward together as a pair in a succession of 'bunny jumps' but that he moves 'left, right, left, right', and that the rider must allow his seat bones to move in the same rhythm and sequence. If you slump a little in the small of your back you will be able to sit more softly and with better depth in the saddle, and you will soon be able to establish a habit of allowing a matching 'left, right, left, right' swing in your hips.

When correcting rider faults, it is essential that the instructor gives a clear, logical explanation of each correction. This will enable the pupil to get the feel of the reason for making the correction as well as feeling the result in the horse's form. For instance, if a diligent pupil is told, 'Get your lower legs *back!*', that pupil will continue to strive to force his or her legs back long after the lesson is finished. When the pupil goes for another lesson a week or a month later, it is probable that the correction will then be: 'Your lower legs are much too far back!' If this counter-correction is given by a different instructor, the poor pupil will suffer from serious confusion!

It is wiser to start with a full but not overlong explanation such as: 'When you use your inside lower leg quite so far back, it will influence solely the horse's hindquarters — either to prevent the horse from swinging them inwards or to move them outwards. I don't believe you really

mean to make either of these aids?!', 'Try to use your inside leg "at the girth" to refreshen the the impulsion and to help the horse to lift the front of his trunk, and to develop a soft bending through the whole of his body around your inside leg.' or 'As you know, a good rider asks for bending with his leg aids rather than with his hands!'

## *A reminder about transitions*

Lunge lessons provide excellent opportunities to improve your prowess at riding good, forward-moving transitions with smooth but clear-cut changes fron one gait to the next. Concentrate on balance, posture, poise — and let your seat bones move with the horse.

The instructor should use, teach and practise many transitions in every lunge lesson, as they are such important factors in every rider's education and as a means of improving a horse's balance, musculature, coordination and form. The instructor must be vigilant and help the rider to keep breathing properly, and to feel the balance, rhythm and muscle work under his seat while freeing himself of any excess tension which may stifle the supple working of any of his joints.

## *Exercises to avoid — they may cause physical damage*

1. All vigorous head-turning exercises, even at walk. The skull should never be jerked upon the neck, as this can have a whip-lash effect and damage the spine.

2. Jerky arm exercises are *out*.

3. Similarly, exercises which are forceful or jerky and which involve the spine are *out*.

4. Stretching the arm upwards before bending down to touch the toes causes an automatic but unwanted hollowing in the small of the rider's back. This will not happen if the rider touches the toe of his or her boot from a position where the hand is hanging softly by the rider's side and goes downwards from there (remembering to come up again, of course).

5. There is another toe-touching exercise which should be avoided – bending down to touch the toe on the opposite side, i.e. touching the left toe with the right hand.

There are two reasons why this exercise should not be used. Firstly it is dangerous if the rider is anywhere near a wall or similar hard obstruction, or a passing ridden horse, as he could injure his head. Secondly, from a postural point of view, the rider's endeavours to reach the opposite toe will invariably pull and twist his seat out of the saddle – not an action to be encouraged.

6. 'Legs out, back and jerk them down!' It is not difficult to understand how much damage this exercise can cause to the rider's hip joints. We only have one pair of hip joints and they have to last us a lifetime!

7. 'Ankle rolling – in, up, out and down.' This is harmful to the whole of the rider's seat and particularly to the hang of the legs. If you try it for yourself, you will feel how these instructions will cause the whole of your leg to turn into a 'hips, knees and toes out' position, which in turn will cause the rider's seat to be excellent for 'bumping trot' but hopeless for 'sitting trot'.

8. Whereas the old cavalry exercise of, 'Body bending forwards and backwards' was fun, as well as being a good means of improving a rider's balance, suppleness and – believe it or not – confidence, in those days saddles did not have the high cantles which are the present vogue and it was perfectly possible to lie back onto the horse's croup. Nowadays, due to the height of the cantle this exercise is not only impossible, it is dangerous, unless it is carried out with the saddle replaced by a folded blanket kept in position by a surcingle.

A 'tail-piece' for this chapter will serve well as a 'tail-piece' for the whole book; it is a reminder to the lunger and to all instructors and trainers . . . and through them to the riders too. It is this. Keep working on the first two of the rider's natural aids or 'helps', those of *thought* and *weight*, and please remember that horses love to be rewarded whenever they have done well ... as do all animals, even humans!

# Index